D1526318

1
LABOR POLICY OF THE UNITED STATES STEEL CORPORATION

STUDIES IN HISTORY, ECONOMICS AND PUBLIC LAW

EDITED BY THE FACULTY OF POLITICAL SCIENCE
OF COLUMBIA UNIVERSITY

Volume CXVI]   [Number 1

Whole Number 258

LABOR POLICY OF THE UNITED STATES STEEL CORPORATION

BY

CHARLES A. GULICK

AMS PRESS
NEW YORK

COLUMBIA UNIVERSITY
STUDIES IN THE
SOCIAL SCIENCES

258

The Series was formerly known as
Studies in History, Economics and Public Law.

Reprinted with the permission of Columbia University Press
From the edition of 1924, New York
First AMS EDITION published 1968
Manufactured in the United States of America

Library of Congress Catalogue Card Number: 68-57568

AMS PRESS, INC.
NEW YORK, N.Y. 10003

To

CHARLES D. TOMKIES
TEACHER AND FRIEND

PREFACE

Those interested in a record of personal experiences in the steel mills are referred to the excellent chronicles of Messrs. Whiting Williams and C. R. Walker. Nothing of that sort is attempted in this study. It purports to be no more than an attempt to gather a quantity of loose fragments into a united whole and to bring a story up to date. With some of these fragments even the most casual reader of the newspapers is familiar; others have remained more obscure. Still others must continue obscure for reasons which will appear. In spite of the objections of "practical" steel men that such work can have no value, there is considerable evidence to the contrary. As a part of that evidence the facts presented in the chapter on hours herein are submitted. In this particular case the records, albeit scattered, are adequate for certain conclusions. Their validity and significance are for the reader to judge.

In securing information it was obviously necessary to appeal directly to the offices of the United States Steel Corporation. Possibly the most widely advertised part of its labor policy is its safety campaign, included in the wider field of "welfare". Consequently, work on this section was undertaken first. Mr. C. L. Close, Manager of the Bureau of Safety, Sanitation and Welfare, and his assistant, Mr. H. A. Schultz, supplied considerable quantities of data and answered a great many questions. The chapters on welfare are, therefore, based very largely on the facts they furnished. When attention was transferred to the question of hours and subsequently to that of wages, requests for information still went through the hands of Mr.

Close, although they were usually passed on to Mr. Filbert,
the Comptroller, or to some other official. As the chapters
on these topics show, the Corporation's records did not contain many of the facts in an available shape; that is, they
were not complete over the entire history of the Corporation,
or they had been kept as individual subsidiary items which
could not be assembled without unwarranted and unjusti-
fiable expense. Such items as the aggregate wage for
manufacturing employees year by year and the fluctuations
in the common labor rate were promptly furnished upon request. For material on the attitude of the Corporation toward labor organizations I was referred to the published
statements of Mr. Gary. Most of the data furnished from
the offices of the Corporation were secured in the spring and
summer of 1922. After an unavoidable delay the work was
completed in the spring of 1924 and submitted to Mr. Close
for criticism.

In his own words those criticisms were that the work was
" prejudiced, unfair to the Corporation, and in many in-
stances not in accordance with the facts ".[1] He offered to
go over " each point in question " if I desired to " set forth
the labor policies of the Steel Corporation in their true light."
In my reply I requested a list of the objectionable items but
this was refused on the ground that there were " too many
of them." In the first five minutes of our conversation of
July 12, Mr. Close stated that he would not cite a specific
instance of my errors unless I would agree to rewrite the
entire book in a different " tone." A few questions made
it clear that in order to find out exactly what he considered
to be wrong I must first pledge myself to reverse all the
major conclusions I had reached. To such a proposal only
one answer was possible. Subsequently, I was accused of
being a member of the Third International and of attempting

[1] Letter of July 7, 1924.

to overthrow the government of the United States. My manuscript convicted me of both in the eyes of Mr. Close. But the most disappointing feature of the interview from my point of view was the refusal of Mr. Close to bring up to date certain data that had been previously supplied. The gaps resulting from this refusal are noted as they appear.

In spite of my request Mr. Close did not submit my manuscript to any other official of the Corporation. He expressed the opinion, however, that they would probably react exactly as he had. For reasons subsequently developed in more detail it is possible that such a reaction was inevitable. These executives are convinced that they are better friends of their employees than the labor leaders. They also believe their methods of handling labor bring in more profits than the method that seems to me more desirable. Since I am more interested in industrial democracy than in large profits for the Corporation, my conclusions rest in part on considerations which must seem either immaterial or beside the mark to the Corporation officials. Some of my statements may be, as Mr. Close declared, inaccurate, though I have made every effort to verify each assertion made and test every conclusion drawn. But the principal ground of difference between us is not, I am convinced, lack of agreement as to the facts but lack of agreement as to their interpretation. Only as Corporation officials substitute for considerations of profit considerations of social service in the broadest sense will the advantages of more democratic labor policies come to be appreciated. It is in the hope of contributing something in this direction that these pages have been written.

I should like to thank individually all those who have assisted me in numerous ways, but their numbers make that impossible. Among those who have aided most materially are Mr. C. L. Close and Mr. H. A. Schultz of the Corpora-

tion, Mr. John A. Fitch of the New York School of Social
Work, Mr. F. E. Johnson of the Federal Council of
Churches, and Professor W. F. Ogburn of Columbia.
Particular acknowledgment is due to Professor R. E. Chaddock for help in certain statistical problems and to Professor
H. R. Seager under whose direction the study was undertaken and carried out. Above all, however, I am indebted
to my wife for aid and encouragement in every stage of the
process.

C. A. G.

New York, August 7, 1924.

CONTENTS

INTRODUCTION

CONDITIONS IN THE STEEL INDUSTRY PRIOR TO THE FORMATION OF THE CORPORATION

As a preliminary to the discussion of the labor policies of the United States Steel Corporation I have thought it desirable to summarize the available data on conditions in the industry prior to the Corporation's formation. Particularly worthy of note are the causal relations between these conditions and the movement toward combination that culminated in this greatest combination of them all.

It may be fairly stated that until 1898 the steel industry was substantially one of competition. It is true that there had been numerous pools and gentlemen's agreements among the producers, such as the steel-rail pool formed in 1887, the wire-nail pool, formally agreed to in 1895, the steel-billet pool of 1896, and the ore pool of the early nineties; but substantially there had been competition. In fact, the keenness of this competition had been the chief cause of the collapse of the agreements that had been made. In one recorded case the agreement was violated within less than 24 hours after its adoption.[1]

A second feature of this earlier situation was that the concerns manufacturing the lighter finished products such as merchant bars, tubes, sheets, tin plate, wire, and wire nails did not produce their own steel but purchased it from the larger steel-making companies.

[1] *Report of the Commissioner of Corporations on the Steel Industry* (Washington, 1911), pt. i, p. 2. Hereafter referred to as the H. K. S. *Report*. (Mr. H. K. Smith was the Commissioner of Corporations at this time.)

In the late nineties combination began with a rush and proceeded at such a pace that in less than three years a very substantial proportion of all the steel-making in the country was in the hands of not quite a dozen large consolidations. The Federal Steel Company, incorporated in September, 1898, was one of the first in this group. It combined the Illinois Steel Company, the Lorain Steel Company, the Minnesota Iron Company, one of the most important of the ore companies around Lake Superior and the proprietor of an ore railroad and a fleet of ore vessels, and the Elgin, Joliet and Eastern Railway. As in many other cases the primary purpose of this combination was to secure integration of productive processes. The concern issued about $100,000,000 of capital stock and controlled approximately fifteen per cent of the steel-ingot production of the United States.

In the following year the National Steel Company was organized by combining the more important of the crude-steel manufacturing companies west of the Alleghenies that were not already in either the Federal Steel Company or the Carnegie Steel Company (Ltd.). The capital stock issue of the National was $59,000,000. Its ingot capacity was only slightly less than that of the Federal concern, viz., twelve per cent of the country's total.[1]

In March, 1900, a third change was accomplished that formally united into the Carnegie Company of New Jersey the H. C. Frick Coke Company and the Carnegie Steel Company (Ltd.). This was more of a reorganization than a true combination of formerly competing concerns, for the Frick and Carnegie interests had been affiliated for a number of years. The capital of the new company was $320,000,000, half in bonds, and it controlled at least eighteen per cent of the ingot production of the United States.

[1] H. K. S. *Report*, pp. 2, 3.

Since the combined capacity of these three combinations, National, Federal, and Carnegie, was nearly half of that of the industry, it might appear that competition had been greatly restricted; but since all three of them were primarily engaged in the manufacture of crude and semifinished steel or of the heavier finished steel products such as steel rails, beams, plates, and bars, it is probably more accurate to consider these earlier combinations as rather intensifying competition than restricting it.

Combination was not confined, however, to companies manufacturing crude, semifinished, and heavy finished products, for at the same time these groupings were being affected a second set of consolidations of companies making more highly finished products was going on. The facts on this development are most concisely expressed in the language of the *Report of the Commissioner of Corporations on the Steel Industry:*

. . . the American Tin Plate Company was organized in December, 1898, with $46,000,000 issued capital stock. It acquired practically every tin-plate concern in the country, giving it an almost complete monopoly of that branch of the industry. The American Steel and Wire Company, organized a month later, with $90,000,000 capital stock, secured all the leading concerns engaged in the production of wire, wire nails, and other wire products. The National Tube Company, formed in June, 1899, with $80,000,000 capital stock, acquired concerns controlling the bulk of the production of iron and steel wrought tubing. A somewhat smaller consolidation of 1899 was the American Steel Hoop Company, capitalized at $33,000,000, a merger of the principal concerns making hoop steel, especially cotton ties.

Early in 1900 the American Sheet Steel Company was organized, with $49,000,000 issued capital stock, to take over the principal manufacturers of steel sheets. The American Bridge Company, formed in April, 1900, with $61,000,000 issued capital stock, controlled the great bulk of the heavy bridge construction business of the country, aside from other structural work. The Shelby Steel Tube Company, a less important concern incorporated in February, 1900, with $13,150,000 issued stock, may also be mentioned. It had substantial control of the seamless tubing industry.

All of these companies were later merged into the United States Steel Corporation.[1]

An important consolidation that did not enter the Corporation was the Republic Iron and Steel Company, organized in 1899 with $47,500,000 issued stock, a consolidation of the principal manufacturers of rolled iron products in the Middle West. Other companies that did not form combinations were expanding their capitalization and their operations at about this time. Among these may be mentioned the Pennsylvania Steel Company, the Cambria Steel Company, the Lackawanna Iron and Steel Company, the Jones and Laughlin Steel Company, the Colorado Fuel and Iron Company, and the Tennessee Coal, Iron and Railroad Company. All of these with the exception of the Tennessee Company have remained without the Corporation.

The principal causes of this earlier combination movement were:

1. The restriction of competition through combination.
2. Integration; that is, the linking up of productive processes through acquisition under one control of raw materials and manufacturing plants (and in some cases transportation facilities) and through extensions and coordination of manufacturing processes.
3. The creation of a great amount of inflated securities.[2]

The first of these was probably the most important.

[1] H. K. S. *Report*, pp. 3, 4.

[2] *Ibid.*, pp. 4, 5.

But the results were not altogether as expected. It had been supposed that competition would be reduced to a negligible factor, but as a matter of fact the combinations recounted above had the paradoxical outcome of increasing competition. The cause is not far to seek. Instead of a competition between individual firms, none of which was particularly dominant, the stage was now set for a battle between giants, each provided with financial resources which only a few years ago had not been even dreamed of.

The second decideratum, integration, had not been accomplished to the extent that had been hoped. It should be recalled that the new combinations were roughly grouped into two classes: a primary group producing almost altogether crude and semifinished steel, of which the Carnegie, Federal, and National Steel Companies were the most outstanding representatives, and a secondary group making the more finished products. The National Steel Company possessed some advantages in having intimate relations with the other " Moore " concerns, the Sheet, Tin Plate, and Hoop combinations. The primary group was dependent upon the secondary for a market, and by the same token the latter upon the former for its " raw " materials. But very shortly it became evident that the companies in the secondary group did not intend to remain in a position of dependence, for as early as 1900 the American Steel and Wire Company, which had previously bought its crude steel from the Federal Steel Company, planned to make its own pig iron and steel; and the National Tube Company, formerly a steady patron of the Carnegie Steel Company, proposed to erect additional blast furnaces and steel works. Numerous other concerns manifested the same tendencies. But the answer to this challenge was easy to find and it was not slow in forthcoming. The Federal Steel Company prepared to take up the manufacture of finished products and in the latter part of 1900 the Carnegie interests announced that they would proceed at once to the erection of an enormous tube mill to take the crude steel that the National Tube Company had decided to cease purchasing. All these concerns, meanwhile, were exerting every effort in an endeavor to secure control of as large quantities as possible of the chief raw materials: iron ore and coking coal.[1]

Such thinly veiled declarations of war were especially disquieting to the financiers who had underwritten (with the hopes of securing promoters' profits) huge quantities of the more or less inflated securities of the earlier combinations. Moreover, since large blocks of the securities were still in the hands of the financiers, and since their value would be greatly depreciated by such a conflict as the impending one gave promise to be, the alarm of their holders is easily understood. On the other hand, it should not be forgotten that this fear was not unmixed with elation, for the shrewdest minds among them saw that although there was a chance for enormous losses, there was also an opportunity for stupendous gains if the situation were only turned in the right direction. Such calculations were based upon the realization that business conditions were steadily improving and that the readiness of investors to support large commercial and financial undertakings was unchecked.

The four financial groups which controlled a very large percentage of the steel industry may be designated as the Carnegie, Moore, Morgan and Rockefeller interests. Though there were some connecting links they may fairly be viewed as distinct. The last of these, the Rockefeller interests, was entirely concerned with the production and transportation of iron ore and hence was not so immediately concerned with the trouble at hand. The other three, however, were the financial backers of the three members of the

[1] H. K. S. *Report*, pp. 9, 10.

" primary " group of steel producers: Carnegie behind the Carnegie Steel Company, Moore behind the National Steel Company, and Morgan behind the Federal Steel Company. To go into the details of the preliminary skirmishing is unnecessary. From a comparison of the report of H. K. Smith, Commissioner of Corporations, and the report of the Stanley Committee of the House of Representatives, both made in 1911, with A. Cotter's *U. S. Steel: A Corporation with a Soul,* I have attempted to summarize very briefly what appear to be the facts in the case.

The Moore interests and the Morgan interests, without any appreciable amount of collusion at first, but later with a fairly definite understanding, were fighting Carnegie. Both of the former, according to the Stanley committee, were heavily over-capitalized. Carnegie, on the other hand, was pictured as almost a paragon of virtue in this respect. He was attempting to do no more than make a fair return on a capitalization built up by forty years of hard work and the process of turning a fairly large proportion of his profits back into the business. His financial position was absolutely sound.[1] If he actually did enter into a price war with these other interests whose immense capitalizations were largely water, he would promptly " lick them to a frazzle," and, again according to the Stanley Committee, no one knew this better than the Morgan interests.[2] Mr. E. H. Gary, at that time president of the Federal Company, was particularly energetic in urging upon Mr. Morgan the advisability of the purchase of the Carnegie concern.

The upshot of the matter was that on March 2, 1901, J. P. Morgan and Company announced the organization of the United States Steel Corporation to acquire control of

[1] *Report* of the Special Committee to Investigate Violations of the Anti-trust Act of 1890 and other Acts, pp. 40, 41.

[2] *Ibid.,* pp. 48-50.

the following concerns: Carnegie Company (of New Jersey), Federal Steel Company, American Steel and Wire Company, National Tube Company, National Steel Company, American Tin Plate Company, American Steel Hoop Company, and American Sheet Steel Company.[1]

At the time of its formation the Corporation controlled 43 per cent of the pig iron production and 66 per cent of the steel ingot and castings production of the United States. Though it has not held its own it still is the dominating figure in the steel industry of the world. As recently as June 2, 1922, Judge Gary testified to the Lockwood committee that the Corporation had a monopoly in certain steel products and produced about half of the supply of many others.[2]

The labor force required to maintain this position during the twenty-three years of the Corporation's existence has fluctuated between 147,000 and 268,000. Of recent years, then, something like 1,000,000 persons in the United States have looked to the Corporation as their immediate source of income, and consequently, from the standpoint of the number of persons affected alone, the labor policy of the Corporation deserves the closest study. In this study attention will be devoted chiefly to the items of hours, wages, attitude toward labor organizations, and welfare. Incident to the

---

[1] H. K. S. *Report*, p. 12.

[2] Judge Gary stated that the monopoly referred to was not illegally acquired, but resulted from the fact that competing concerns did not produce some lines. He did not explain why this situation existed. *New York Times*, June 3, 1922. (This Lockwood Committee, more accurately described as the New York state joint legislative committee on housing, conducted an investigation of the housing problem in New York in 1922. It was alleged before it that the United States Steel Corporation could manufacture steel at from $3 to $5 a ton less than its competitors, and that these competitors existed only on sufferance of the Corporation. Judge Gary was called in to testify concerning these statements.)

discussion of the Corporation's attitude toward labor organizations is included a sketch of the labor relations in the industry prior to 1901. Possibly the facts stated there might be better included in this introductory chapter, but the writer believes that to do so would involve considerable repetition and lost motion in later sections and consequently has confined this introduction to matters of business and financial organization.

CHAPTER I

HOURS OF LABOR

FOR two generations the steel industry has been notorious for its long hours. The fundamental process in the industry, the conversion of iron ore into pig iron in the blast furnaces, is necessarily a continuous process. When a furnace is once put in blast it is not put out except for a complete cessation of work. In the words of the 1911 report of the Bureau of Labor,

In the blast furnace department there are strong technical reasons for continuous operation not only night and day but also 7 days a week. Any long interruption of operations unless very elaborate preparations for "banking" are made, is not only detrimental to the product but may result in serious injury to the furnace. . . Even if technically possible, the process of banking as often as once a week requires the unproductive burning of such tremendous quantities of coke that it is unlikely that such a method is commercially profitable.[1]

Consequently, blast furnace workers must be on duty twenty-four hours in the day and seven days in the week. The simplest method of working continuously, naturally adopted in the early days of the industry, was to operate with two shifts of men, each working seven twelve-hour turns a week,

---

[1] Neill, Charles P., Commissioner of Labor, *Report on Conditions of Employment in the Iron and Steel Industry in the United States* (Washington, 1913), vol. iii, p. 164. (Hereafter referred to as "Neill.")

[22

the shifts alternating every seven or fourteen days from day
to night work. Quite often the shifts were eleven and
thirteen or ten and fourteen rather than exactly twelve and
twelve, but any of these combinations is referred to as " the
twelve-hour day," since that is what they average.

Such hours were in themselves severe enough, but they
carried with them a still greater evil, the " long turn."
When the change was made from day to night duty, the
shifts had to work eighteen or twenty-four hours continuously. Then if a relief man failed to appear or if the crew
was short, some men had to remain on duty. This overtime
work was so common that in the *Report on the Conditions
of Employment in the Iron and Steel Industry* made in 1911
the following statement appears: " Continuous periods of
36, 48, and 60 hours of employment are fairly usual at the
——furnaces." [1]

An earlier record, the annual report of the Bureau of
Labor for 1904, shows that from 1890 to 1903 one hundred per cent of the blast furnace employees in the occupations recorded worked eighty-four hours a week, that is,
seven turns of twelve hours each. The same hours were
extended to several other departments, not because there was
the same necessity for them that existed in the blast furnaces,
but because it was the easiest thing to do. Statistics of
hours by departments always show that the blast furnace
employees suffer most from excess hours, with the Bessemer
converter and open hearth workmen only a trifle more favored. This is explained by the absolute continuousness of
blast furnace operations and by the larger proportion of unskilled labor in them.

Prior to August, 1923, excessive hours were probably the
chief complaint of the workers in the industry; they were
certainly the chief indictment which its critics brought

[1] Neill, *op. cit.*, vol. iii, p. 202.

against it. Thirty to forty years ago, strange as it may seem, the objections of the workers were directed against the introduction of the three-shift system. This point is clearly made in J. S. Robinson's history of the Amalgamated Association of Iron, Steel and Tin Workers. Speaking of the " boiling " operations in an iron mill during the period 1885 to 1894 he notes that " the Amalgamated has succeeded in resisting the demand of the manufacturers for three turns in union plants; there are, however, a few non-union mills employing three shifts." Of the sheet and tin plate mills, he says:

As early as 1885 sheet mills were allowed to work three shifts of 8 hours, providing the crews did not exceed the specified limit of output. This, however, was not conceded by the union without some opposition. . . . When the tin business began to prosper about 1890 the union allowed the use of the three-turn system of operation of tin mills.[1]

Within the last fifteen years the volume of protest against the prevailing hours in steel grew larger. In the opinion of the Commission of Inquiry of the Interchurch World Movement, which investigated the steel strike of 1919, this protest was unavailing; in fact, in its *Report on the Steel Strike of 1919* [2] figures are submitted to show that between 1914 and 1919 hours actually increased. In the following pages it is my purpose to examine the trend of hours throughout the history of the United States Steel Corporation, in so far as the available statistics will permit, to state the attitude of the Corporation on the matter, and to determine, if possible,

[1] Robinson, J. S., *Amalgamated Association of Iron, Steel and Tin Workers* (Baltimore, 1917), pp. 107, 110, 111. The basis of the objections to the three-shift system was the belief of the men that their pay would remain at the same rate per hour, and that consequently their total earnings would be reduced.

[2] *Cf.*, pp. 54, 71, 72.

the extent to which its good intentions have materialized and to what extent they have gone the way of so many other good intentions.

During the first six years after the formation of the Corporation there are no comprehensive statistics on hours for the industry at large, much less for the Corporation. For reasons that will be made clear [1] the use of any figures intended to cover the industry to represent the situation in Corporation plants is unwise and will be avoided. This is particularly true of the meager data available for the early years. Consequently, the point of departure for this chapter will have to be the following resolution concerning hours passed on April 23, 1907, by the finance committee of the Corporation.

On motion, it was voted to recommend to all subsidiary companies that Sunday labor be reduced to the minimum; that all work (excepting such repair work as can not be done while operating) be suspended on Sunday at all steel works, rolling mills, shops, quarries, and docks; that there shall be no construction work, loading or unloading of materials.

It is understood that it is not at present practicable to apply the recommendation to all departments, notably the blast furnaces, but it is desirable that the spirit of the recommendation be observed to the fullest extent within reason.[2]

The effects of the resolution can not be definitely established, for within six months the steel industry was struck by a depression that slowed down production to such an extent that even repair work could be done without any appreciable amount of Sunday labor.

[1] See footnote p. 30.

[2] Neill, *op. cit.*, vol. iii, p. 165. It should be noted in passing that the Pittsburgh Survey was just getting under way at this time and that 1907 was the first year in which the Bureau of Labor attempted to secure comprehensive statistics on wages and hours in the steel industry.

Two years later, however, the demand for steel had so far recovered that by November, 1909, practically every steel plant in the country was working. The report of the Commissioner of Labor to the Senate in commenting on the situation says that the Corporation mills were no exception to the rule, ". . . for in the rush of business the resolution of the finance committee regarding Sunday work was forgotten." [1]

In February, 1910, the workers of the Bethlehem Steel Corporation went on strike, their principal grievance being the long hours, including the frequent exaction of excessive overtime. On March 20, 1910, the United States Senate ordered an investigation of this strike. On the next day, March 21, 1910, Judge Gary sent the following telegram to the presidents of all subsidiaries:

Mr. Corey, Mr. Dickson, and I have lately given much serious thought to the subject matter of resolution passed by the finance committee April 23, 1907, concerning Sunday or seventh-day labor. Mr. Corey has written you on the subject within a day or two. The object of this telegram is to say that all of us expect and insist that hereafter the spirit of the resolution will be observed and carried into effect. There should and must be no unnecessary deviation without first taking up the question with our finance committee and asking for a change of the views of the committee, which probably will not, under any circumstances, be secured. I emphasize the fact that there should be at least 24 continuous hours' interval during each week in the production of ingots.[2]

This did not affect blast furnace operations.

The next official action was taken at the stockholders' meeting of April 17, 1911, at which Mr. Charles M. Cabot introduced the following resolution:

[1] Neill, *op. cit.*, vol. iii, p. 166.
[2] *Ibid.*, p. 166.

Resolved, That the chairman shall forthwith appoint a committee of not more than five persons from the officers, or stockholders, of this corporation, to investigate and report to the finance committee, as soon as may be, but not later than October 1, 1911, as to the truth of the statements contained in a certain article appearing in the March number of the American Magazine, under the title " Old Age at Forty," and that such report, together with such comment as said finance committee may desire to add thereto, shall thereupon be printed and mailed to the stockholders of this corporation.[1]

In spite of the desire for prompt action evidenced by the wording of the resolution, the report of the committee was not rendered until April, 1912. Among other things it said :

Whether viewed from a physical, social, or moral point of view, we believe the 7-day week is detrimental to those engaged in it. . . . we are strongly of the opinion that no matter what alleged difficulties in operation may seem to hinder the abandonment of the 7-day week, they must be met.

     *   *   *   *   *   *

. . . we are of the opinion that a 12-hour day of labor followed continuously by any group of men for any considerable number of years means a decreasing of the efficiency and lessening of the vigor and virility of such men.

The question should be considered from a social as well as a physical point of view. When it is remembered that the 12 hours a day to the man in the mills means approximately 13 hours away from his home and family—not for one day, but for all working days—it leaves but scant time for self-improvement, for companionship with his family, for recreation and leisure.[2]

---

[1] *Investigation of Strike in Steel Industries, Hearings before the Committee on Education and Labor, United States Senate* (Washington, 1919), p. 230. (Hereafter referred to as *Senate Hearings, 1919.*)

[2] Neill, *op. cit.*, vol. iii, p. 161.

Acting upon this report, the finance committee of the Corporation in May, 1912, passed several resolutions stating that the seven-day week, the long turn, and any excessive workday in general should be eliminated. Specifically, a committee composed of the chairman of the finance committee and the president of the corporation was appointed ". . . to consider what, if any, arrangement with a view to reducing the 12-hour day, in so far as it now exists among the employees of the subsidiary companies, is reasonable, just and practicable." [1]

This second committee reported that nothing could be done toward relieving the situation " unless competing iron and steel manufacturers will also enforce a less than twelve-hour day." Consequently, Mr. Cabot introduced at the 1913 meeting of the stockholders a resolution requesting the directors of the Corporation " to enlist the co-operation of the steel manufacturers of the United States in establishing the eight-hour day in continuous twenty-four hour process." The resolution was tabled. [2]

In the meantime great progress was made in limiting the amount of seven-day work throughout the industry and particularly in the Corporation plants. The Bureau of Labor report cited before credits the Corporation with having practically abolished the seven-day week from its blast furnaces, always the strongest hold of long hours, by March, 1912. [3]

For 1911, a date ten years subsequent to the formation of the Corporation, it is possible for the first time to secure any fairly comprehensive statistics on hours which apply only to the Corporation; all reports prior to that time were made for the steel industry as a whole. During the hearings

[1] Neill, *op. cit.*, vol. iii, p. 162.
[2] *Survey*, May 3, 1913, pp. 165, 166.
[3] Neill, *op. cit.*, vol. iii, p. 168.

before the Congressional committee which investigated the Corporation in 1911 a mass of figures was submitted showing the results of the efforts to do away with seven-day work. Condensed and tabulated these facts were as follows: [1]

TABLE I

THE TWELVE-HOUR SHIFT AND SEVEN-DAY WEEK IN U. S. STEEL CORPORATION SUBSIDIARIES IN 1911

Name of Subsidiary Company	No. of men employed (average)	No. of men on 12-hour shift	Per cent of men on 12-hour shift	Men working 7 days a week
H. C. Frick Coke Co......	22,640	475	2.1	Less than .1 of 1 per cent.
Universal Portland Cement Co...................	2,550	892	35.0	5 per cent.
Oliver Mining Co...	13,390	1,138	8.5	Very few.
Lorain Steel Co..........	1,456	72	5.0	None.
American Bridge Co......	11,577	583	5.0	Watchmen only.
American Sheet and Tin Plate Co..............	20,221	2,614	12.9	2 per cent.
American Steel and Wire Co....................	24,595	4,919	20.0	None in blast furnaces or steel mills.
Tenn. Coal, Iron and Rr. Co.	12,656	2,898	22.9	Very few.
National Tube Co.........	17,319	4,037	23.31	None.
Carnegie Steel Co........	31,761	17,150	54.0	3.4 per cent.
Illinois Steel Co..........	17,450	10,470	60.0	Less than 5 per cent.
Total	175,715	45,248	25.75	Less than 5 per cent.

As thus presented the figures show that the Commissioner of Labor was no more than just in giving the Corporation a clean bill of health on the seven-day week. Although the number of employees on this schedule was not made public, it is probable for the years 1911, 1912, 1913, 1914, and

[1] *Hearings before the Committee on Investigation of the U. S. Steel Corporation* (Washington, 1911), vol. v, pp. 3284-88. (Hereafter referred to as *Stanley Hearings*, 1911. Mr. A. O. Stanley was chairman of the committee.)

possibly 1915 that they did not average as much as five per cent of the Corporation's employees.[1]

On the other hand the facts as to the prevalence of the twelve-hour day are somewhat obscured. Apparently only 25.75 per cent of the Corporation's employees are subjected to such long hours as compared with the 42.58 per cent which the Bureau of Labor found in the steel industry in May, 1910. This difference may be interpreted as representing the degree to which the Corporation was leading the industry as a whole, but I am convinced that such was not the case.

[1] The Interchurch Commission of Inquiry came to quite different conclusions. On page 72 of the *Report on the Steel Strike of 1919* are the following statements: " Statistics from Bureau of Labor Statistics Bulletin 218 (Oct., 1917) reveal what actual successes were accomplished by the Corporation in ' eliminating ' seven-day work. Seven-day workers in blast furnaces were: (p. 17) 1911, 89 per cent; 1912, 82 per cent; 1913, 80 per cent; 1914, 58 per cent; 1915, 59 per cent. . . . The best year's figures show that the Corporation never achieved even a half-reform." Take the year 1912 for which comparisons of absolutely definite nature can be made. The government publication cited by the Interchurch Commission states that in 1912, 82 per cent of the blast furnace men worked seven days a week; the *Report on the Conditions of Employment in the Iron and Steel Industry*, vol. iii, p. 168, states that the Corporation had practically eliminated seven-day work from its blast furnaces in 1912. The explanation of the discrepancy is simple. In the first place, Bulletin 218 covers the industry at large, not the Corporation alone. Second, the Interchurch Commission forgot to state that in 1912 the data for blast furnaces in the wages and hours bulletin were based on a sample of 36 plants. For Neill's report, which I have cited, a complete census of every furnace in blast was made and this complete census shows a total of 156 furnaces instead of 36. The statistical table presented on page 169 of this report shows that 9,801 employees of the Corporation were relieved of seven-day work; that 4,216 employees of independent concerns were relieved of such work; but that 18,960 employees of other independents were not so relieved. In one plant of the Corporation 28 per cent of the blast furnace men still worked seven days a week; in 26 plants of the Corporation seven-day work was practically abolished. In view of these facts, the Interchurch statement that " the best year's figures show that the Corporation never achieved even a half-reform," is manifestly an error.

In the first place the government figures were based on the employees in the blast furnaces, steel works and rolling mills alone. Thus the administrative, clerical, and selling forces included under the employees of the Illinois Steel Company or the Carnegie Steel Company were omitted from the government figures. Second, by the same limitation of the employees classified the Bureau of Labor excluded all coal miners, coke workers, railroad workers, etc., who are included in the Corporation's figures. Thus the impossibility of directly comparing the data supplied by the Corporation with the government report of 1910 is apparent; but if the H. C. Frick Coke Company, the Universal Portland Cement Company, and the Oliver Mining Company are eliminated, some of the difficulties are avoided. In the remaining subsidiaries the percentage of twelve-hour workers is 31.16; however, it must be remembered that in this computation are included a number of clerical and administrative workers. Consequently, a conservative estimate would place the twelve-hour men among the Corporation's steel workers at a minimum of 35 per cent in 1911.

From 1910 to 1914 a continued shortening of the " average full-time hours per week " in the industry as a whole brought them in most of the departments to the lowest levels that up to that time had been achieved. This highly desirable result came from two causes: the sincere work done by the Corporation and some of the independents in reducing the amount of seven-day work, and the severe depression that hit the steel business in 1914. A glance at the table on page 57 of employees in the manufacturing properties in each year of the Corporation's operations will show just how severe that depression was. 1902, 1903, 1904, 1905 and 1908 are the only years in which the number of employees was smaller, and 1904 and 1908 were themselves bad years in the steel business.

Thus eight years after the resolution of 1907 and five after the peremptory telegram of March, 1910, considerable progress in the alleviation of long hours had been made. The last positive statement that can be made concerning conditions in the Corporation's subsidiaries prior to the war period carries us no farther than March, 1912, but because of the depression of 1914 and because of the ascertainable facts for the industry as a whole in that and the preceding year, it seems safe to say that for five years the seven-day week was greatly reduced in the Corporation's plants. On the other hand, as pointed out, next to nothing was accomplished in reducing the twelve-hour day, and at least 35 per cent of the manufacturing employees (25.75 per cent of total employees) were on that schedule.

For the next three and one-half years, that is, to August, 1919, the facts on hours in the Corporation are concealed by a cloud of ignorance equaled in blackness only by the clouds of smoke which poured from its stacks. Steel was on a boom that dwarfed every other period of activity in its history and on the face of it all other considerations seemed submerged in the mad rush for production and profits. Even the Bureau of Labor Statistics failed to secure any information for the years 1916 and 1918, but the data for 1917 and 1919 are sufficient to tell the story for the industry in general. In the ten departments of the industry for which data were compiled the following figures show the percentage of employees whose average full-time hours per week were 72 and over.[1]

---

[1] Computed from Bureau of Labor Statistics Bulletin No. 305, *Wages and Hours of Labor in the Iron and Steel Industry: 1907 to 1920* (Washington, 1922), pp. 8-10. These percentages are for "selected occupations;" those for "all occupations" were not published for 1919.

TABLE II

PERCENTAGES OF EMPLOYEES WORKING 72 HOURS AND OVER PER WEEK
BY DEPARTMENTS, 1914 AND 1919

	1914	1919
Blast Furnace	78	84
Bessemer Converters	60	65
Open Hearth Furnaces	81	89
Puddling Mills	1	1
Blooming Mills	70	68
Plate Mills	47	75
Standard Rail Mills	78	78
Bar Mills	6	16
Sheet Mills	5	3
Tin Plate Mills	1	1

These figures it must be remembered are based on samples
which are intended to represent the industry at large.

For the four departments in which the seven-day week
was the most prevalent the percentage of men on that
schedule in 1914 and 1919 follow.[1]

TABLE III

PERCENTAGES OF EMPLOYEES WORKING THE SEVEN-DAY WEEK
BY DEPARTMENTS, 1914 AND 1919

	1914	1919
Blast Furnaces	58	80
Bessemer Converters	12	5
Open Hearth Furnaces	31	28
Blooming Mills	5	12

[1] Bureau of Labor Statistics Bulletin No. 305, pp. 5 and 6. The figures
are for "selected occupations."

The increase in blast furnaces seems bad, but in 1920 the percentage had dropped to 54, the lowest on record for the industry. On the other hand the percentage in Bessemer converters had risen to 23 in 1920. On the whole, however, it seems fairly clear that at no time during the war did the seven-day week become quite so prevalent as it had been before 1910 when the Corporation and the American Iron and Steel Institute began a drive against it. The permanent gain must not be over-estimated; it was, in fact, discouragingly small in view of the time that had passed, but some advance had been made.

Finally, some idea of the trend of hours may be gained by comparing the average full-time hours per week in each department for 1914 with those for 1919. This comparison is not so satisfactory because the Bureau presents only relative figures, not the actual hours on which they were based. Very briefly this table [1] shows that between the years mentioned average full-time hours had increased in four departments and decreased in six. With this very brief survey of what was going on in the industry as a whole, let us now return to the situation in the Corporation plants.

As stated before the working hours of Corporation employees were almost completely obscured in the months of intense war-time activity. In September, 1919, however, things began to happen which threw considerable light on the points in question. First came the strike involving practically the entire steel industry; second, the Senatorial investigation in which Judge Gary was the spokesman for Corporation and independents alike; third, the Interchurch Inquiry; fourth, the investigation for the Cabot Fund by Mr. John A. Fitch and associates of the situation in the summer of 1920; and, finally, various official statements from the offices of the Corporation at irregular intervals during the period since the strike.

---

[1] See Bureau of Labor Statistics Bulletin No. 305, p. 3.

It will be recalled that by the Corporation's own figures, backed by the investigation of the Bureau of Labor, the seven-day week was practically done away with in 1911. On April 7, 1922, during a conversation with me in his office, Mr. C. L. Close of the Corporation's Bureau of Safety stated emphatically that seven-day work had been done away with by January 1, 1921, except in rare cases of repair work that had to be done in emergencies. Even in such cases he insisted that the workers who were called on for extra time were later compelled to take a day off so that in a period of as long as say ten weeks every man would have had ten days off. In the conversation of July 12, 1924, mentioned in the preface, I asked Mr. Close whether this rule of compelling men to take days off was still in force in every plant of the Corporation. He reiterated even more emphatically that such was still the rule and that it was enforced. It is possible that the situation in at least one plant was not known by Mr. Close, but I have it from a reliable source that in the Edgar Thomson works at Braddock, Pennsylvania, the seven-day week was the usual practice from the latter part of October, 1923, until the first of May, 1924, in at least the blast furnace and open hearth departments.[1]

In the first conversation mentioned Mr. Close had admitted that there was considerable seven-day work during the war but emphasized war needs as justifying it. Following the same line Mr. Gary told the Senate Committee that the reason for reintroducing the seven-day week was that "the Government was clamoring for more and more steel all the time." Directly after the armistice the Secretary of War notified the Corporation "to stop all Sunday work,

[1] My informant, who prefers to remain anonymous, is a graduate of Harvard and was a graduate student with me at Columbia in 1921-22. He was employed in the Edgar Thomson works during the period cited above as a common laborer. During this time he and the entire gang in which he was regularly worked seven days a week.

overtime, and night work on Government contracts, effective immediately." [1] In a letter of January 30, 1920, to the Interchurch Commission Mr. Gary said, "During the war, at the urgent request by government officials for larger production, there was considerable continuous seven-day service in some of the departments." [2]

Mr. Gary should know more about the reason for reintroducing the seven-day schedule than any outsider, but the following extract from the petition of the Lackawanna Steel Co. for exemption from the one day of rest law of New York state suggests that the change began prior to our entry into the war and was prompted by the enormous demand for steel. No other inference can be drawn from the fact that the petition was presented in 1916, the year before we entered the war.

We are advised that the chairman of the United States Steel Corporation several years ago, while labor conditions were entirely different from those obtaining at the present time, gave instructions quite peremptory in character to all the subsidiaries of that company requiring them to follow out the one day of rest principle and warning them that any deviation from the published instructions would result in dismissal from office. We have, therefore, directed our investigations to these subsidiaries and state, without fear of successful contradiction, that *the corporation is now disregarding the one day of rest in seven principle* which it so strongly advocated several years ago and which it in the past, in good faith, earnestly strove to put into practice. It, too, has felt the shortage of men, and owing to the great and pressing demand for its product no longer observes the practice which its chairman promulgated. Having taken so firm a position, it is not strange that it is diffi-

---

[1] *Senate Hearings*, 1919, p. 179.

[2] Commission of Inquiry, the Interchurch World Movement, *Report on the Steel Strike of 1919* (New York, 1920), p. 69.

cult to get heads of subsidiaries to admit that the published rule has become a dead letter. When labor conditions become normal the corporation will doubtless return to an observance of the rule. So far as we can ascertain, the rule was only observed by the corporation during the years when the employees of this company had far more time off than the one day of rest statute requires.[1]

From these statements it is of course impossible to make any statistical comparisons, but it can not be questioned that the seven-day week in Corporation plants assumed large proportions in part of 1916 and all of 1917, 1918, and 1919. In view of the facts already presented for the industry in 1919 and 1920 it is probable, however, that conditions never became as bad as they were in 1910. On the question of the seven-day week, then, some permanent advance seems to have beeen made; but for the year 1920 at least, this advance seems to have been made at the cost of putting more men on the twelve-hour shift, a fact to be immediately developed.

Fortunately, the information on this point applying only to the Corporation is somewhat more definite and complete. The following chronological summary records the success of the Corporation in reducing this excessive schedule. It is made up from published statements of Corporation officials, in the last three cases, of Judge Gary.[2]

The reader will note that the figures are presented by months in certain years rather than for entire years as would be desirable. The inadequacy of this method is realized,

[1] Interchurch, *Report on the Steel Strike of 1919*, p. 75. Quoted from an article by Professor John R. Commons in the *American Labor Legislation Review* for March, 1917, p. 147. The Lackawanna's petition was refused.

[2] *Stanley Hearings*, 1911, vol. v, pp. 3284 *et seq.*; *Senate Hearings*, 1919, p. 157; *Statement by Elbert H. Gary, Chairman, United States Steel Corporation at Annual Meeting, April 17, 1922*, pp. 7, 8.

but efforts to secure more comprehensive information on hours from the Corporation have been fruitless because it has apparently been the policy of the Corporation to compile comprehensive data, not regularly from year to year, but only for emergencies such as the Stanley Hearings in 1911 or the Senate Hearings in 1919.

TABLE IV

PER CENT OF TOTAL EMPLOYEES WORKING TWELVE-HOUR SHIFT AT PERIODS INDICATED

Month	Year	Per cent
....	1911	25.75
August	1919	26.50
October	1920	32.00
March	1922	14.00

Since these data were all computed on the total number of employees they are adequate for such a comparison as just made, but including as they do miners, railroad workers, clerical help, administrative and selling forces, the effect of the method of computation is to minimize the percentage of *bona fide* steel workers who work this long day. This being the case, the percentages should be recomputed on the basis of the number of employees in the manufacturing companies. It is apparent that such recomputations should be made by ascertaining the total number of employees of the manufacturing subsidiaries in each of the months in question and the number of these working twelve hours and taking the latter as a percentage of the former. However, the total employees in manufacturing subsidiaries are available for March, 1922, only; and the twelve-hour employees in manufacturing subsidiaries for August, 1919, only. Until more adequate data can be secured, then, the recomputation will

have to be confined to those two months. In 1922 it shows
that approximately 18 per cent of the total manufacturing
employees were on twelve hours.[1] In 1919 the figures are
on a slightly different basis, i. e., the twelve-hour workers
in manufacturing subsidiaries are taken as a percentage, not
of total manufacturing employees, since that figure was not
available, but of " wage-earners in manufacturing." This,
of course, is almost the ideal method of presentation, since
it eliminates the administrative and clerical forces to a considerable extent as well as the coal miners, coke workers,
and transportation employees. These data show 169,853
wage-earners in manufacturing subsidiaries of whom 66,-
711 were on a twelve-hour turn. The percentage was
39.27.[2] A comparison of this with Judge Gary's 26.5 per

[1] In this recomputation it has been assumed that all 12-hour men are
employed in the manufacturing subsidiaries. The Corporation officials
object to this on the ground that the figures for 12-hour men include
workers outside manufacturing subsidiaries and that consequently my
percentages are too high. They were unable to furnish the detailed
figures necessary to correct what is admitted to be a defect except for
August, 1919. These showed a total of 69,284 men on twelve hours, of
whom 66,711 were in the manufacturing subsidiaries. Manifestly, the
error is not great. (A letter of May 14, 1923, from Mr. G. K. Leet of
the Corporation to the author supplied the figures for 1922. Those for
1919 appeared in the *Survey* for March 5, 1921, p. 785, and were likewise
furnished by the Corporation.)

[2] *Survey*, March 5, 1921, p. 785. The Interchurch Commission computed that 52.4 per cent of the Corporation's employees worked the
12-hour shift in 1919. (See the discussion on pp. 47, 48 and 49 of its
Report.) It reached this conclusion on the basis of the testimony to
the Senate of Superintendent Oursler of the Homestead works of the
Carnegie Steel Co., plus the letters of Mr. Gary to the Commission
explaining this testimony. For the Homestead works the Interchurch
computation is doubtless correct, but since these works are only a part
of the Carnegie Steel Co., which is itself only one, though the chief
one, of the manufacturing subsidiaries, and since the 1911 figures show
that the Carnegie Co. was at that time exacting more 12-hour work
than any other subsidiary save one, it seems to me that the Interchurch
conclusion is based on too slight a foundation.

cent of total employees, including presidents of subsidiaries, general managers, clerical help, coal miners, railroad and steamship employees, etc., etc., shows rather definitely how misleading his statements to the Senate were when construed, as they were by most persons, to represent a percentage of *steel* employees.

But all percentages tend to hide an important fact. The twelve-hour day is an individual matter; it is worked by individual men who have wives and children and homes from which they are kept twelve and a half to fourteen hours a day. What had happened to the actual number of individuals who for more than half their working lives can not even be in the same building with those they hold most dear? To what extent had the Corporation's efforts to reduce hours decreased the number of men on this schedule? In 1911 there were 45,248 on the twelve-hour shift; in October, 1920, there were approximately 85,000.[1]

Thus after ten years of " peremptory " telegrams, stockholders' resolutions, protestations of belief in shorter hours to Congressional committees, and vigorous objections to the " interference " of " outsiders " who " do not understand the situation " the number and percentage of twelve-hour workers were materially larger.[2]   The drop in March, 1922,

[1] It is impossible to state exactly the number. Judge Gary told the stockholders on April 17, 1922, that in October, 1920, 32 per cent of the " total employees " of the Corporation were working twelve hours a day. But, as usual, actual figures were not stated. If 32 per cent of the average total employees for the year is taken the result is 85,550. The smallest number of employees in any month in 1920 was 261,037, in May. (*Annual Report for 1920*, p. 29.) If 32 per cent of this is taken the result is 83,553. Obviously the approximate figure of 85,000 is close enough, absolute accuracy being impossible.

[2] To this conclusion Corporation officials take vigorous exception on the following grounds:

1. Before and after our entry into the war primary departments, where the 12-hour day centers, were enlarged disproportionately to finishing departments so that the per cent of 12-hour men in the industry

was very largely the result of poor conditions in the industry, although some of it was caused by the introduction of machinery that permanently displaced twelve-hour men.

At this point notice must be taken of certain developments without the mills that had considerable importance in bringing the whole question to an issue. As noted above the investigations of Mr. Fitch and associates in the summer of 1920 were financed by the Cabot Fund. There were already some twenty concerns that were operating on three shifts in those departments such as the blast furnace and open hearth where in most establishments the long day still prevailed. The results of these experiments would serve as a fitting complement to the investigation just mentioned, and so the Cabot Fund undertook this also, engaging Mr. Horace B. Drury for the purpose. The results of his work were reported to a joint meeting of several engineering societies

was enlarged despite material reductions in their numbers and percentages within these primary departments.

2. The fact that months rather than years were used makes it impossible to draw any fine comparisons because of the fluctuation of these percentages from month to month.

The first point seems to me to be completely irrelevant. The net result of the developments in the plants had been to increase the percentage of 12-hour men, and to my mind the net results are the vital item.

The second objection would be better taken if data were offered to substantiate any different inference from the one drawn in the text. The main points I wish to stress are clearly admitted in letters to me from the Corporation in the statements following. "The figure 32% on which you base your computation represents our maximum percentage except perhaps for a few months in 1918." "As I stated to you in my last letter, although actual computations have not been made, the percentage during certain months of 1918 was undoubtedly higher than that for August, 1919, as was the percentage for October, 1920, which Judge Gary gave as the highest for which we have any record." (Letters of May 14 and June 1, 1923. The "32%" is for October, 1920.) It is apparent that the Corporation has not maintained an adequate record of the men on the 12-hour schedule, and that what data exist support the position I have taken.

on December 3, 1920, and published in the *Bulletin of the
Taylor Society* for February, 1921. After discussing the
extent of the twelve-hour day, the reasons for it, and the
reasons for abandoning it, Mr. Drury proceeded to summarize the experiences of the plants that had made the
change. The most interesting facts for us are that he found
" practically all " the managers of three-shift plants " glad
that they made the change," and that he agreed with previous
estimates made by the Bureau of Labor that the cost of
making the change should not add more than about three
per cent to the cost of making steel.[1] Subsequently, Mr.
Drury was engaged by the Cabot Fund to make a second report on the methods by which the change from two to three
shifts could best be made. During this investigation he
convinced himself that under proper and perfectly possible
management the three-shift system would mean lowered, not
increased, labor costs.[2] More comprehensive than either of
the reports mentioned was that of the Federated American
Engineering Societies on *The Twelve-Hour Shift in Industry*. In addition to steel the investigation included other
metal industries, glass, cement, lime, brick, pottery, chemical
industries, sugar, salt, petroleum, paper, flour, and many
others. The work was done by Mr. Drury and Mr. Bradley
Stoughton. As in the preceding reports the financial aid
came from the Cabot Fund. It is obviously impossible to
summarize the 300 pages of the report here, although one
definite statement can be made: from the technical engineering viewpoint the long shift is wasteful and unwise. Moreover, it should be noted that the engineers secured the en-
dorsement of the report in a foreword by the late President
Harding, for it is almost certain that the interest aroused in

[1] *Bulletin of the Taylor Society*, February, 1921, pp. 23 and 27.
[2] *Cf. The Technique of Changing from the Two-Shift to the Three-
Shift System in the Steel Industry*. (Proof-sheets of May, 1922), p. 78.

him at this time prompted him to call for May 18, 1922, a conference of steel producers on the twelve-hour day. At the conclusion of the conference, which included forty-one steel executives, the President, and Secretaries Mellon, Hoover, and Davis, Judge Gary gave the following statement to the press:

After full and frank discussion in which it was apparent all favored abolition of the twelve-hour day, if and when applicable, it was unanimously resolved that a committee of five from the steel industry be appointed by the President of the Iron and Steel Institute to make careful and scientific investigation and report to the steel industry their conclusions and recommendations.[1]

On May 26, at the annual meeting of the Iron and Steel Institute, Judge Gary announced the following members of the investigating committee: Charles M. Schwab, Chairman of the Bethlehem Steel Corporation; James A. Farrell, President of the United States Steel Corporation; W. L. King of the Jones and Laughlin Steel Corporation; A. C. Dinkey, President of the Midvale Steel and Ordnance Company; James A. Campbell, President of the Youngstown Sheet and Tube Company; James A. Burden of the Burden Iron Company; L. E. Block of the Inland Steel Company; John A. Topping, Chairman of the Republic Iron and Steel Company.[2]

The report of this committee was made May 25, 1923, and was signed for the Corporation by Mr. Gary and Mr. J. A. Farrell, the president. Without doubt this document is one of the most astonishing in industrial history. The committee claimed that it " had made a very careful and painstaking study of the facts and figures developed." Outstanding statements in the report include the following:

[1] *New York Times*, May 19, 1922, p. 1.

[2] *Ibid.*, May 27, 1922, p. 15.

Apparently the underlying reason for the agitation which resulted in the appointment of this committee was based on a sentiment (not created or endorsed by the workmen themselves) that the twelve-hour day was an unreasonable hardship upon the employees who were connected with it; that it was physically injurious to a large percentage of the employees; and that it interfered with family associations essential to the welfare of the children; that for these reasons it was, in a sense, opposed to the public interest.

Whatever will be said against the twelve-hour day in the steel industry, investigation has convinced this committee that the same has not of itself been an injury to the employees, physically, mentally, or morally. Whether or not, in the large majority of cases, twelve-hour men devote less time to their families than the employees working less hours is perhaps questionable.

*   *   *   *   *   *

. . . large production at low cost, for sale at fair prices, the entire world is more dependent upon at the present time than ever before.

Our investigation shows that if the twelve-hour day in the iron and steel industry should be abandoned at present, it would increase the cost of production on the average about 15%; and there would be needed at least 60,000 additional employees.[1]

The committee believed it impossible to secure these men

[1] *New York Times*, May 26, 1923. This estimate of a 15 per cent increase in cost is nothing short of preposterous. Estimates made by the Bureau of Labor in 1910 that "the complete introduction of the 8-hour system would probably increase the cost of production and the selling price of the most highly finished products of the industry that are now made under the 12-hour system only 3 per cent" (Neill, *op. cit.*, vol. iii, p. 185) were borne out by the experiences of the plants studied by H. B. Drury after they had made the change. In a conference with President Coolidge Judge Gary admitted that the Institute's estimate had been 33 per cent too high when he stated that the increase had been 10 per cent. He added that the "industry hoped to offset this increase in due time through plant improvements and better labor efficiency." (*New York Times*, January 23, 1924.)

and laid the responsibility " partly with the American Congress " and the immigration laws. Consequently, the report continues, " the committee cannot at this time report in favor of the total abolition of the twelve-hour day." In other words, the matter was indefinitely postponed.

This announcement, viewed in many quarters as tantamount to a refusal to meet popular sentiment as voiced by President Harding, raised a storm of denunciation throughout the country. The labor papers were particularly vehement against the " sell-out " as they characterized it, and even the most conservative organs could find little or nothing in the report to approve. On June 6 the Federal Council of the Churches of Christ in America united with the Catholic Welfare Council and the Central Conference of American Rabbis, bodies representing in round numbers 50,000,000 persons, in a statement which is given in full because it covers so completely the case against the Institute's report.

The report of the Committee on Proposed Total Elimination of the Twelve-Hour Day appointed by the American Iron and Steel Institute shatters the public confidence that was inspired by the creation of the Committee a year ago at the request of the President of the United States. It is a definite rejection of the proposal for the abolition of the long day. The public demand in response to which the Committee was appointed is set aside as a " sentiment " which was " not created or endorsed by the workmen themselves." The testimony of competent investigators, including eminent engineering societies, is ignored, and the conclusion is put forth without supporting data that the twelve-hour day " has not of itself been an injury to the employees, physically, mentally or morally." This statement is made in face of the fact that the committee of stockholders of the United States Steel Corporation, appointed in 1912 to investigate this matter, expressed the opinion " that a 12-hour day of labor, followed continuously by any group of men for any considerable number of years means a decreasing of the efficiency and lessening of the vigor and virility of such men."

Objection to the long day because of its effect on the family life of the twelve-hour workers is disposed of in the report with the complacent comment that it is questionable whether men who work shorter hours actually spend their leisure time at home. This is an unworthy and untenable argument which will be bitterly resented by the millions of home-loving workingmen in America.

The Steel Institute's Committee contends that the workmen themselves prefer the long hours. Undoubtedly there are those who will voluntarily work long hours to their own hurt, but the Committee's contention is chiefly significant as showing that workmen whose only choice is between abnormally long hours of labor and earnings that are insufficient to maintain a family on a level of health and decency, naturally adopt the more arduous alternative.

The plea that a shortage of labor makes impracticable the change from two to three shifts of workmen, affords but a meager defense. The shortage of labor was not the reason for the failure to abolish the long day two years ago when the public waited expectantly for such a salutary step on the part of the United States Steel Corporation. At that time there was appalling unemployment which could have been in large measure relieved in steel manufacturing districts by introducing the three-shift system in the steel industry. The task may be more difficult now than it would have been then, but a past delinquency affords no release from a present moral obligation.

The Steel Institute's Committee finds that the entire cost of a change to the eight-hour day would have to be paid by the consumers of steel, disregarding the possibility of some proportionate contribution out of the earnings of the industry. Thus the safeguarding of profits becomes a consideration superior to that of the wages and hours of the workers, and the willingness of the public to pay higher prices is made a condition of the accomplishment of a fundamental reform.

The Steel Institute's Committee finds that there are " questions of high importance "- involved in this whole matter, which, they assert, have no moral or social features. "They are economic," say the steel manufacturers; "they effect the pecuniary interest of the great public, which includes but is not confined to employers and employees." This divorce between the "moral" or "social" elements of a problem and its economic aspects runs counter to the teaching of religion. It exalts a misconceived "law of supply and demand" to a position of equal authority with the law of justice. It excuses inhumanities in the name of economic necessity. Furthermore, it overlooks an important series of demonstrations within the steel industry and elsewhere, of the practicability and superior advantages of the three-shift system. These demonstrations confirm in practice what no honest mind can question in principle —that bad morals can never be good economics.

The one redeeming feature of the Committee's report is the intimation that it is not final. The public has waited long for the fulfillment of a virtual promise from the industry that the twelve-hour day would be abandoned. The public expects the initiative to be taken by the United States Steel Corporation. It is a task that presents admitted difficulties, but none that a powerful corporation which has accumulated an enormous surplus should find insurmountable. The forces of organized religion in America are now warranted in declaring that this morally indefensible regime of the twelve-hour day must come to an end. A further report is due from the Iron and Steel Institute—a report of a very different tenor.[1]

A few days later the Federal Council released for publication a letter from Mr. J. F. Welborn, president of the Colorado Fuel and Iron Company. The change from twelve- to eight-hour shifts was made in this concern November 1, 1918. The letter shows that both officials and workmen are satisfied with the change and includes the following significant statements:

[1] Federal Council of the Churches of Christ in America, *The Twelve Hour Day in the Steel Industry* (Bulletin No. 3), pp. 76-78.

The trend of production per man hour, with unimportant exceptions, has been upward since the adoption of the eight-hour day; and in every department of our steel manufacturing operations, from blast furnace to the wire mill, our production per man hour is now greater than it was when all of these activities were operating on the twelve hour shift. Comparing these results of the last few months with periods of similar production when basic rates were ten per cent lower than current rates and the working time twelve hours per day, we find that almost without exception our labor cost per ton is lower than in the earlier periods.

President Harding wrote to the Iron and Steel Institute on June 18 expressing his regret and disappointment over the action taken May 25 and requesting a pledge from the Institute that it would abolish the long day when labor conditions warranted the step. To this a group of the directors replied on June 27 that they recognized the public sentiment against the twelve-hour day, and that the change would be made " when, as you state it, ' there is a surplus of labor available.' " [1]

On the preceding day, June 26, the Federal Council had issued a research bulletin on " The Twelve Hour Day in the Steel Industry," a compilation from government bulletins, steel officials' statements, the Engineers' report on *The Twelve-Hour Shift in Industry,* and other sources. The evidence presented was overwhelmingly against the long day.

During all this time countless news items and editorials had appeared in dailies, weeklies, and monthlies commenting on the Institute's report, the statement of the church bodies on that report, the Welborn letter, etc., etc., so that the steel industry had been under constant fire for a month. The first intimation of any weakening of the position taken on

[1] These letters were not published until July 6, 1923. See the *New York Times* of that date.

May 25 appeared in Judge Gary's statement to the press on
July 6.

I can't say exactly when the United States Steel Corporation
or any other company will get rid of the twelve-hour day
entirely, but I can positively state that they will begin to act
in that direction very soon and be very diligent in their efforts.[1]

A week later " a prominent director of the Iron and Steel
Institute " stated that "the leading steel companies of the
country are busily engaged in reshaping their personnel for
the purpose of bringing about the entire elimination of the
twelve-hour day." On the same day a conference of mill
foremen in Mr. Farrell's office in New York was announced
as forthcoming.[2] On July 26 the presidents of the Corporation's subsidiaries met in New York to discuss the question, and on August 3 it was announced that on the preceding
day the directors of the Iron and Steel Institute had adopted
plans for the "total elimination" of the twelve-hour day
"as rapidly as the supply of labor will permit." [3]

The use of the formula bringing in the supply of labor
still left some doubts as to when the "elimination" would
begin, but for the Corporation these were dispelled by the
announcement on August 9 that on August 16 part at least
of the twelve-hour departments at Pittsburgh, Gary, and
other points would be changed to three eight-hour shifts.
In the newspaper story carrying this announcement was the
following statement: "The plan will be started with a full
realization that a labor shortage will result and curtailment
of output will follow, officials stated." Just eleven days
later the following statement, also under a Pittsburgh date
line, appeared:

[1] *New York Times*, July 7, 1923.

[2] *Ibid.*, July 15, 1923.

[3] *Ibid.*, August 3, 1923.

The new 8-hr. day in the steel mills is attracting workmen who
have never had any connection with the industry, and mill managers and employment agents today were predicting that it
would not be long until the labor shortage indicated last week
would be overcome and all the plants would be in full operation
on the three-shift schedule.[1]

The September 20, 1923, issue of the *Iron Age* contained
an article on "One Month's Progress in Reducing Hours."
Although the difficulty of making definite statements was
recognized and pointed out, it was possible to make the
following generalization: "In the Pittsburgh-Wheeling-
Youngstown district a careful casting up of estimates made
by the different companies would indicate that about half of
the total number of men formerly engaged on the longer
turn are now working 8-hour turns."[2] This, of course,
included Corporation and independent plants. References
to Corporation subsidiaries show that the eight-hour shift
had been adopted in all continuous processes at the Cleveland
plants of the American Steel and Wire Company,[3] and that
in the Carnegie Steel Company's works at Youngstown only
a few men were still on twelve hours.[4] On September 24
announcement was made that several finishing units of the
Carnegie's plant at Pittsburgh had been put on eight hours.[5]

The *Iron Age* for January 3, 1924, contained another
summary of progress, the facts having been ascertained by
its representative in the various districts. The results may
be summarized as follows:

1. In the Pittsburgh-Wheeling-Youngstown district
the

[1] *Cf.* the *New York Times* for Aug. 9, 1923, and Aug. 20, 1923.
[2] P. 750.
[3] P. 772.
[4] P. 773.
[5] *Iron Age*, Sept. 27, 1923, p. 861.

elimination of the 12-hr. day in the steel industry is at least 70 per cent completed among the independent plants as an average and almost 100 per cent accomplished in the Steel Corporation units in that area. At the inauguration of the movement on Aug. 16, the Steel Corporation moved with a great deal more speed in the adoption of the late President Harding's suggestion than did the independent companies. . . .

As the *Iron Age* points out, however, the conclusion must not be drawn " that the record of the Steel Corporation finds no parallel among independent companies," for at least three of them in the Youngstown district began reducing hours before the Corporation did and " these companies now are little, if any, behind the Steel Corporation in the actual application of the shorter day."

2. Chicago district: ". . . the 12-hr. shift has been entirely eliminated in all United States Steel Corporation plants and with very few minor exceptions is now a thing of the past also in all other steel works. . . ."

3. Birmingham district: " Elimination of the 12-hr. day is being tried out, or rather being put into execution, only by the United States Steel Corporation subsidiaries in this district. . . ."

4. Cleveland district: " The American Steel & Wire Co. was the first to adopt the three-shift plan. . . ."[1] (This company is a Corporation subsidiary).

From all of these statements it is clear that the Corporation, once committed to the change, went about it in an energetic and thorough-going fashion. It should be noted, moreover, that the foregoing results were accomplished in four months despite the predictions of the *Iron Age* in September that a year would be required. Of course, the change was facilitated by the slackened demand for steel ar ' ' .

---

[1] *Iron Age*, Jan. 3, 1924, pp. 35, 39, 40.

favorable labor situation resulting therefrom, but in point-
ing this out it is not intended to detract from what has been
accomplished. So far as can be ascertained there has been
no attempt to hamstring or discredit the movement on the
part of Corporation officials; to the contrary, in fact. What
will happen when steel begins to boom again remains to be
seen, but for the present we should be gratified by the well-
nigh complete manner in which the reform has been accomplished.

On the attitude of managers and superintendents to the
change the *Iron Age* found that although a few managers
were still cautious in their statements, the great majority in
all districts were enthusiastic in their praise of the results
to date. They believed the workmen were better satisfied
and that the original grumblings at less total earnings are
now quieted by the realization of the advantages of more
leisure and of not being so badly tired by a day's work.
Conversations with the men justified this opinion according
to the representatives of the *Iron Age*. All the managers
agreed that the men were more efficient, a result which no
doubt arises partly from the fact of lessened employment.[1]

In concluding this chapter on hours, I should state that
I have purposely refrained from inserting a mass of figures
from the government bulletins on wages and hours in steel
for the reason that they are intended to represent the industry, not the Corporation. The Interchurch *Report* misused
these figures,[2] and I wish to avoid that mistake. The
sociological and psychological consequences of the long day
have not been treated because that work has been well done
by Mr. Fitch in *The Steel Workers* and in his numerous
magazine articles, particularly in the *Survey* for March 5,
1921; by Whiting Williams in *What's on the Workers'*

[1] *Iron Age*, Jan. 3, 1924, pp. 34-41, *passim.*
[2] See footnote, p. 30.

Mind, and in the *Survey* for March 5, 1921; by C. R.
Walker in *Steel, The Diary of a Furnace Worker;* by the
Interchurch Commission in the *Report on the Steel Strike
of 1919.* Nor has any attempt to demonstrate the practicability of the three-shift system been made. It was super-
fluous. Since 1910 at least the evidence has been rapidly
accumulating which demonstrates the invalidity of the
position taken in the Iron and Steel Institute's Report of
May 25, 1923, that the change would involve a fifteen per
cent increase in costs and an approximately fifty per cent
increase in men in continuous processes.[1]

On the basis of the available facts it is impossible to
formulate conclusions of a desirable definiteness. As pointed
out before, the Corporation has made no attempt to record
statistics of hours from month to month or year to year,
but has been content to collect such figures only for the
emergencies of a Congressional investigation, a change in
methods of computing wages, or a statement to the Iron and
Steel Institute or to the stockholders. Thus we have the
spectacle of one of the largest and richest corporations in the
world, under fire for at least fifteen years because of the
twelve-hour day, knowing accurately how many men it employed on that schedule for only four months of the period!
Even worse than the inadequacy of the data is the method
of their presentation. In the four cases cited twelve-hour
men were referred to as a percentage of " total employees,"
despite the fact that all government figures on hours in the
industry with which it is desirable to make comparisons omit

[1] Neill, *op. cit.,* vol. iii, pp. 171-192; "Three-Shift System in the
Steel Industry," by H. B. Drury, in the *Bulletin of the Taylor Society*
for February, 1921; "The Technique of Changing from the Two-Shift
to The Three-Shift System in the Steel Industry," a Report to the Cabot
Fund in 1922 by H. B. Drury; *The Twelve-Hour Shift in Industry,*
Federated American Engineering Societies, 1923, particularly pp. 219-293,
in the report on the steel industry by Bradley Stoughton.

all administrative, clerical, and selling forces. In the one case, August, 1919, in which the manufacturing employees were separated from the " total " that total was given as 266,966 to Mr. Fitch though Judge Gary had testified to the Senate that it was 261,180.[1] These facts raise the question of the desirability of requiring corporations whose gross income exceeds some established minimum to operate under a federal license or charter which should provide for reports to the government on this and similar matters. The personal opinion of the writer is that some such requirements should be made, an opinion that derives considerable support from facts developed in the chapter on wages.[2]

A second conclusion, more definite in character, is that the Corporation appears to have led the industry in eliminating seven-day work. This is true, I believe, in spite of its

---

[1] *Cf.* the *Survey* for March 5, 1921, p. 785, and *Senate Hearings*, 1919, p. 157.

[2] It should be noted that Mr. J. A. Farrell, president of the Corporation, put himself on record in 1911 as being in favor of the federal government assuming " such supervision of corporations engaged in interstate traffic as will result in full and clear publicity of their general operations, their receipts and expenditures and profits and losses, in order to protect investors and the people generally." *Stanley Hearings,* 1911, vol. iv, p. 2697. Mr. Gary's testimony to the same committee indicated that he was in favor of federal licensing, perhaps federal incorporation, but his chief reason seems to have been that he wanted his corporation, and others, to know more definitely what was permitted by the government. Court decisions in cases involving an interpretation of the Sherman anti-trust act had manifestly left him in a quandary as to exactly where the line would be drawn. *Ibid.,* vol. i, p. 249-252. Before the Senate Committee in 1919 Mr. Gary reiterated his statements of 1911 on federal licensing and suggested the appointment of a commission which ". . . should have supervision over the management of the corporation, including even the labor questions . . . ," provided that all contested points might be subject to review in federal courts. *Senate Hearings,* 1919, p. 216. Mr. Gary emphasized the fact that he was speaking here as an individual, not as a representative of the Corporation.

admitted lapses in 1909 and during the war, and in spite of
the deviation in the Edgar Thomson plant in the winter of
1923-'24 brought out above.

Third, the Corporation lagged behind the smaller independents in abolishing the twelve-hour day,[1] but deserves
considerable credit for the energy it displayed between
August and December, 1923, in accomplishing the reform.

Fourth, the Corporation has moved toward the reform of
excessive hours only when business was poor or when the
spur of outside criticism was appied. The " peremptory "
telegram the day after the Senate had ordered an investigation of the strike against excessive hours in the Bethlehem
plants; the appointment of the committee to report on the
truth of J. A. Fitch's " Old Age at Forty "; the drop in the
percentages of excessive hours in " lean " years; the complete reversal in tone and action in the summer of 1923; all
of these force the conclusion that reforms in hours have
waited on steel demand and a sufficiently aroused public
sentiment.

[1] See the *Bulletin of the Taylor Society* for February, 1921; the
Survey for March 5, 1921; and the Engineers' report, *The Twelve-Hour
Shift in Industry.*

CHAPTER II

WAGES

The wages paid by an industrial corporation are the most vital part of its labor policy. Whatever may be true of the hours, working conditions, opportunities for advancement, etc., etc., the central question is, "How do they pay?"; and if wages are high, much else will be tolerated by employees and general public alike. High wages, however, must be understood to mean high real wages; that is to say, the writer is not interested in a comparison of the wages paid by the Corporation with those paid by its competitors in the steel industry or with those paid in other industries. The more important comparison is that between wages and living costs. What facts are available for making this comparison?

In the first place it is evident that the periodic bulletins of the United States Bureau of Labor Statistics on hours and wages in the steel industry cannot be used directly because the data presented were collected from the industry at large. The greater part of the data relating to the Corporation alone is presented in the following tables.

TABLE V

EMPLOYEES AND WAGE BILLS OF THE U. S. STEEL CORPORATION,
1902-1923 [1]

Year	Total employees (average)	Total wage and salary bill	Average annual wage	Employees of mfg. properties (average)	Wage and salary bill for mfg. properties	Average annual wage in mfg. properties
1902	168,127	$120,518,343	$717	125,326	$92,236,357	$736
1903	167,709	120,763,896	720	123,397	91,672,387	741
1904	147,343	99,778,276	677	110,864	76,541,536	690
1905	180,158	128,052,955	711	130,614	94,778,669	725
1906	202,457	147,765,540	729	147,048	109,255,784	743
1907	210,180	160,825,822	765	151,670	116,863,613	770
1908	165,211	120,510,829	729	118,557	88,380,225	745
1909	195,500	151,663,394	776	138,865	111,066,443	800
1910	218,435	174,955,139	800	154,563	126,338,522	817
1911	196,888	161,419,031	822	140,118	117,582,120	839
1912	221,025	189,351,602	856	161,774	140,204,292	866
1913	228,906	207,206,176	905	165,277	152,602,049	923
1914	179,353	162,379,907	905	131,616	121,654,760	924
1915	191,126	176,800,864	925	140,875	133,537,938	948
1916	252,668	263,385,502	1,042	187,289	200,022,469	1,068
1917	268,058	347,370,400	1,296	198,711	263,895,383	1,328
1918	268,710	452,663,524	1,685	199,029	345,268,192	1,735
1919	252,106	479,548,040	1,902	188,550	374,203,502	1,984
1920	267,345	581,556,925	2,173	200,991	445,946,832	2,219
1921	191,700	332,887,505	1,736	133,963	232,111,722	1,732
1922	214,931	322,678,130	1,501	150,847		
1923	260,786	469,502,634	1,800	180,727		

[1] Compiled from the annual reports of the Corporation except that the wage and salary bill for the manufacturing subsidiaries was furnished by the comptroller of the Corporation, that the Corporation has not published an "average annual wage" for every year and that consequently for some years it had to be computed, and that the average for manufacturing employees was computed for each year. Moreover, the averages are shown only to the nearest dollar. The Corporation was unwilling to bring these data up to date as explained in the preface.

TABLE VI

HOURLY RATES PAID TO COMMON LABOR IN THE PITTSBURGH AND CHICAGO
DISTRICTS

Effective on	Rate	Effective on	Rate
Jan. 1, 1900	$.15	Oct. 1, 1917	$.33
June 1, 1902	.16	April 16, 1918	.38
Jan. 1, 1904	.145	Aug. 1, 1918	.42
April 1, 1905	.155	Oct. 1, 1918	.42*
Jan. 1, 1907	.165	Feb. 1, 1920	.46*
May 1, 1910	.175	May 16, 1921	.37*
Feb. 1, 1913	.20	July 16, 1921	.37
Feb. 1, 1916	.22	Aug. 29, 1921	.30
May 1, 1916	.25	Sept. 1, 1922	.36
Dec. 16, 1916	.275	April 6, 1923	.40
May 1, 1917	.30	Aug. 16, 1923	..

* With 50 per cent additional for time over 8 hours. These rates were supplied by the Comptroller of the Corporation, but the rate since August 16, 1923, the Corporation was unwilling to furnish as explained in the preface.

From the first table it appears that the average wage received by the 168,000 (average) employees of the Corporation in 1902 was $717. The inadequate character of this figure becomes obvious upon analysis of the detailed summary showing that of the 168,000 employees

122,000 received less than $800,
44,000 received from $800 to $2,500
1,300 received from $2,500 to $5,000
150 received from $10,000 to $20,000
15 received $20,000 and over.[1]

An approximate average for the second group, those receiving $800 to $2,500, is $1,100.[2] For the higher income

[1] *Stanley Hearings*, 1911, vol. vi, p. 4537. It will be noted that those receiving from $5,000 to $10,000 were omitted from the data supplied to the Stanley Committee.

[2] This figure is, as stated, an approximation. It was reached as fol-

groups it is too difficult to secure even an approximate dis-
lows. The group receiving $800 to $2,500 forms 26.2 per cent of the
total. It has been impossible, of course, to find a detailed distribution
of incomes for a group receiving the range $800 to $2,500 for the year
1902 in which that group formed 26.2 per cent of the total. In Neill's
report of 1910, vol. iii, p. 550, is a table of full-time weekly earnings of
172,409 steel employees. If employment of 50 weeks is assumed the
rates $16 to $50 are equal to annual earnings of $800 to $2,500. Between
these two rates 27.4 per cent of the total distribution falls and the
average annual earnings of the group would be $1098. If 45 weeks em-
ployment are assumed the rates $18 to $50 are equal to $810 to $2,250
in annual earnings. (For a discussion of the basis for using 45 weeks
see p. 63. The last group in the classification is "$50 and over" and
includes only .4 of one per cent of the total, so that in spite of the fact
that the upper limit is slightly below the $2,500 of the Corporation's
table, the per cent of employees thus omitted is insignificant in percentage terms.) In the group receiving $810 to $2,250 are included 18.9
per cent of the total and the average wage would be $1088. It is to be
noted that I have converted weekly wage rates into approximate annual
earnings and that the distribution covers 1910 conditions.

A second set of estimates of 1910 incomes is found in W. I. King,
Wealth and Income of the People of the United States, pp. 228 and 229.
These estimates are family income, not individual earnings, and show
45.13 per cent of the distribution in the group receiving $800 to $2,500;
but making allowances for these differences the average of $1167 is
remarkably close to those computed from the Bureau of Labor's report.

Another basis for the approximate figure of $1100 is found in the
work of Professor Henry L. Moore on the so-called "Dewey Report"
on "Employees and Wages" as ascertained in the 1900 census. Professor Moore's results were published in the *Political Science Quarterly*,
vol. 22, the particular table here used appearing on p. 67. In this table
the weekly wage rates paid in 30 industries were grouped in one dollar
intervals from "$2-$3," "$3-$4," on to "$49-$50" and "$50 and over."
If 50 weeks are assumed as a year, 13.77 per cent of the workers received
annual amounts of $800 to $2,500, and the average wage in the group
was $1045; if 45 weeks constituted a year, 8.72 per cent of the total were
in the $800 to $2,500 group, and the average was $1046.

Finally, the weekly wage rates in the Dewey Report for iron and
steel workers alone are available. Since these data are confined to
iron and steel workers and since they represent conditions for 1900, they
are in these respects more useful in attempting to find a figure approximately true in 1902. Assuming, as before, a 50-weeks and a 45-weeks
year, computation shows that in the former case 17.5 per cent of the
total were in the $800 to $2,500 group and received an average wage

tribution and so the minima will be used. From these it can be computed that at least $300,000 went to the fifteen highest paid employees of the Corporation in 1902, that at least $150,000 was paid to the next group, and that at least $3,250,000 was paid to the 1,300 persons receiving from $2,500 to $5,000. To the 44,000 receiving $800 to $2,500, approximately $48,400,000 was paid. The remainder of the total wages and salary bill, divided by the 122,000 men who received less than $800, gives an average for that group of $560. It must be noted that because of the use of minima in the three highest groups and the omission of the $5,000 to $10,000 group, this figure of $560 is somewhat too high. It would be interesting to apply the foregoing method to later years, but since the details given in the table were compiled for 1902 only, and since the comptroller of the Corporation has stated that it would be impossible to secure them now for other years, this method of splitting up the unsatisfactory aggregate figures given above must be abandoned.

Since 1912 the Corporation has also published annually two figures purporting to represent the " average earnings per employee per day " : one " exclusive of " and the other

of $1227; and that in the latter, 12.5 per cent fell in this group and received an average wage of $1241.

The net results of my efforts to find an average for the income group $800 to $2,500 are then the following averages: $1045 and $1046 from Professor Moore's work, $1088 and $1098 from Neill's report, $1167 from King's *Wealth and Income of the People of the United States,* and $1227 and $1241 from the 1900 census volume on " Employees and Wages." These figures are all approximations; three of them refer to 1910 conditions; six are computed from individual wage rates and one is a set of estimates of " family " incomes; but in spite of all these limitations which are freely granted, I still believe they justify the approximation of $1100 given in the text. That this estimate is a conservative one is indicated by the fact that the data from the Dewey Report on iron and steel workers alone for 1900 indicated an average for this $800 to $2,500 group of $1227 for a year of 50 weeks and of $1241 for a year of 45 weeks.

" including " the " general administrative and selling force ".
These are, of course, as inadequate as the average annual
wage and present the further difficulty that in order to secure the result published by the Corporation it is necessary
to assume, for example, that there were 311 working days
in 1912, but only 305 in 1914 and 307 in 1915.

Another possibility is suggested in the Interchurch *Report
on the Steel Strike of 1919*. In the chapter on wages the
Report attempted to divide the manufacturing employees of
the Corporation into three groups: unskilled, semiskilled,
and skilled, to ascertain what percentage of the annual wages
bill went to each of the groups, and thus to secure an average figure representing the annual wage of the individuals
in each group.[1] In reaching its conclusions the *Report* assumed that the percentage divisions of the three classes of
labor true in 1910 for one plant employing 6,372 workmen
were true in 1918 and 1919 for all the plants of the Corporation, and that the proportion of the total wages bill
going to each of these groups was the same in 1918 and
1919 as in 1910. These assumptions were made despite the
facts that for the industry at large the *Report on the Conditions of Employment in the Iron and Steel Industry in the
United States,* cited by the Interchurch *Report* to substantiate its percentages, gives a quite different set of percentages,[2] and that in commenting on the stability of these proportions the statement is made that

The whole tendency of the industry is to greatly increase the
proportion of the production force formed by this semiskilled

[1] See the *Report*, ch. iv, pp. 85-98, and p. 270.

[2] *Cf.* Neill, *op. cit.*, vol. i, p. xxxii, and vol. iii, p. 80. The former
shows that in the industry 49.69 per cent of the employees were unskilled, 26.71 per cent semiskilled, and 23.6 per cent skilled; the latter
that in one plant 38.1 per cent were unskilled, 31.5 per cent semiskilled,
and 30.4 per cent skilled. The Interchurch *Report* based its calculations
on this one plant.

class of workmen. They are displacing both the skilled and the unskilled workmen, though at present the displacement is largest among the unskilled, as the function of most of the machinery recently developed is to perform work formerly done by unskilled labor rather than to eliminate the necessity for skilled employees.[1]

In the latter part of the war boom the Corporation installed a great deal of machinery which still further altered the proportions in its plants of these groups.

Since it is manifestly impossible to use the same proportions over any considerable part of the twenty-three years of the Corporation's history, the next step is to attempt to follow the changes from year to year. But this line of attack is completely blocked because the Corporation has never divided its workmen into skilled, semiskilled, and unskilled groups, and because, except for the month of August, 1919, it does not know how many or what proportion of its employees were receiving the common labor rate of pay. Consequently, the attempt to reduce to intelligible terms the mass of totals presented in the Corporation's annual reports must be abandoned.

But even if it is impossible to separate these annual wage totals by finding what percentage of the men were in each of three, or more, wage groups, and what percentage of the total went to each in a given year, may it not be possible to build up a figure that will represent what the man on the common labor rate could expect to earn in a year? The unknown item is, of course, the number of hours the man worked in a year. For 1910, however, this can be stated with passable accuracy, since from data presented in the 1910 survey of working conditions it is possible to compute that the " average customary working hours per week " of

[1] Neill, *op. cit.*, vol. iii, p. 81.

the unskilled group were almost exactly 72,[1] and since the same survey states that "Taking these various causes of unavoidable lost time into consideration it seems probable that during a prosperous year like 1910 the average employee does not have an opportunity to work more than 45 weeks during the year. . . ."[2] This means then that an average unskilled workman could expect to make $556 in 1910.[3] Because of the fluctuations in business from year to year and the fluctuations of the Corporation's practices concerning hours it is impossible to use for any other years the figures approximately true for it in 1910 except as avowed estimates. And from all of the above facts it seems clear that it is impossible to reach for any considerable group in the Corporation's employ an accurate figure for annual earnings.

These expedients failing, the most fruitful comparison seems to be that between changes in the common labor rate

[1] The method of reaching this figure was as follows. The first volume of the report presented summary tables of hours for every productive occupation in the various departments. The unskilled occupations were selected in all departments, the "average customary working hours per week" for each occupation multiplied by the number of individuals working those hours, and the total hours divided by the total employees. There was, of course, considerable difference in the average hours of the unskilled group in the various departments. The highest average was in the blast furnaces: 78.35 hours a week; the lowest in the puddling mills: 58.41 hours. For the data from which these averages were computed see Neill, op. cit., vol. i, pp. 42, 73, 101, 125, 139, 171, 197, 218, 237, 252, 283, 306, 329.

[2] Ibid., vol. iii, p. 214.

[3] A result secured by multiplying 72 hours per week by 45 weeks to the year at the rate of .1716 an hour. The table on page 58 shows that for the first four months of 1910 the rate was .165; for the last eight, .175. It is apparent at once that figures collected for the industry on hours per week and weeks per year are being combined with a wage rate from Corporation plants. This method would not be justifiable except for the facts that the 1910 survey was so nearly complete and that the Corporation at that time had not accomplished a great deal in reducing hours.

and those in the cost of living. It should not be forgotten that the fluctuations in the common labor rate are particularly significant in the steel industry since a large percentage (49.69 in 1910) of the men are paid that rate and since the wages of the semiskilled group fluctuate in close accord with those of the laborers.[1] In making the comparison suggested at least two methods will be employed. The first is that utilized by Mr. I. M. Rubinow and later by Professor Paul Douglas and Miss F. Lamberson, viz., to measure changes in the cost of living by the fluctuations of the Bureau of Labor's index of retail food prices.[2] This basis has been adopted because of the importance of food in the workingman's, particularly the common laborer's budget; because of the demonstration in the articles just cited of the closeness with which living costs and food prices fluctuated, at least until 1916; and because of the practical fact that it is the only continuous set of data covering the period since the organization of the Corporation that is available. The inaccuracies involved in using an index of food prices as a measure of changes in the cost of living since about 1915, and more particularly since June, 1920, are discussed and largely corrected on pages 66-68. In computing the following two sets of index numbers, however, an average of the years 1901 to 1905 inclusive has been used in preference to the customary 1913 base. 1901 is used because the Corporation began operations then; the five-year period because a wider base

[1] *Cf.* Neill, *op. cit.*, vol. iii, p. 251.

[2] *Cf.* I. M. Rubinow, "The Recent Trend of Real Wages," *American Economic Review*, vol. iv, p. 793, December, 1914; and P. H. Douglas and F. Lamberson, "The Movement of Real Wages," *American Economic Review*, vol. xi, p. 409, September, 1921. The one essential difference in method is that I have used the Bureau's index as printed, whereas in the articles cited it was recomputed using only the 15 articles for which prices exist for every year since 1890. The differences in results, however, are negligible.

than a single year is desirable. The question at issue is: Has the United States Steel Corporation advanced wages sufficiently to keep their levels equal with the new levels reached by the cost of living? For the moment it is immaterial whether or not the aggregate wages a laborer could expect to earn in a given year were adequate for a " minimum," a " saving," a " comfort," or any other level of existence. The significant comparison here is that between the levels of wages and prices in any given year and the average level for the period 1901-1905; a comparison clearly indicated by the following sets of index numbers.

TABLE VII

COMPARISON OF CHANGES IN THE CORPORATION'S COMMON LABOR RATE WITH THOSE IN THE COST OF LIVING AS MEASURED BY THE RETAIL PRICES OF FOOD

[AVERAGE 1901-1905=100]

Year	Corporation common labor rate	Cost of living
1901	98.2	96.2
1902	102.0	100.2
1903	104.8	100.2
1904	95.0	101.6
1905	99.8	101.6
1906	101.5	105.6
1907	108.0	109.6
1908	108.0	112.2
1909	108.0	119.0
1910	112.4	124.3
1911	114.6	123.0
1912	114.6	131.0
1913	129.5	133.6
1914	131.0	136.3
1915	131.0	135.0
1916	156.8	152.4
1917	196.0	195.1
1918	262.0	224.5
1919	321.0	248.6
1920	348.5	271.3
1921	271.4	204.5
1922	209.6	190.0

From them it is apparent that in 1901 the wage index and the food index were practically identical; that in 1902 they rose at almost exactly the same rate; that the wage index rose slightly in 1903 while that for food remained constant; that the wage cut in 1904 ran counter to a small rise in the cost of food; and that from 1904 to 1915 the rate of increases in wages never brought the level of wages measured from the 1901-1905 base up to the level of food prices measured from the same base. In 1916 wages increased a little faster than food costs and in 1917 a little slower, so that the index for wages is slightly above in 1916 and almost identical with that for food in 1917. From 1918 to 1920, however, increases in wages were at a greater rate than those in food prices, and in 1921 and 1922 the fluctuations of decreases followed by increases in wages have never brought their level below that of food prices, at least so long as the comparison is made on a calendar year basis. Actually, wage rates were forced below food prices on August 29, 1921, a fact shown by putting the index numbers on a monthly basis.

But as suggested above, the validity of measuring movements of living costs by fluctuations of the food index alone for the period since 1915, and more particularly since June, 1920, is open to serious question. In addition to the index of retail food prices the Bureau of Labor Statistics has for several years published an index of changes in the cost of living in the United States as shown by the average cost of living in a number of cities. This index includes clothing, housing, fuel and light, furniture and furnishing, and miscellaneous items in addition to food. From December, 1915, to June, 1919, the percentage increase of food prices on a 1913 base was greater than the percentage increase in the cost of living as shown by the combined items. For December, 1919, and June, 1920, the food increase and the cost of living increase were almost identical, but by De-

TABLE VIII

COMPARISON OF CHANGES IN THE CORPORATION'S COMMON LABOR RATE
WITH THOSE IN THE COST OF LIVING AS MEASURED BY THE
COMPOSITE INDEX OF THE BUREAU OF LABOR STATISTICS

[1913=100]

Month and Year	Corporation common labor rate	Cost of living *
Dec., 1914	101.1	103.0
Dec., 1915	101.1	101.1
Dec., 1916	132.7	118.3
Dec., 1917	166.8	142.4
Dec., 1918	247.7	174.4
June, 1919	247.7	177.3
Dec., 1919	247.7	199.3
June, 1920	271.0	216.5
Dec., 1920	271.0	200.4
May, 1921	244.1	180.4
Sept., 1921	151.7	177.3
Dec., 1921	151.7	174.3
Mar., 1922	151.7	166.9
June, 1922	151.7	166.6
Sept., 1922	182.0	166.3
Dec., 1922	182.0	169.5
Mar., 1923	182.0	168.8
June, 1923	202.2	169.7
Sept., 1923	....	172.1
Dec., 1923	....	173.2

Monthly Labor Review, February, 1924, p. 94 [310].

cember, 1920, food prices had dropped until they were only
78 per cent above the 1913 average, whereas the total cost
of living was 100.4 per cent above the 1913 average. This
disparity became more pronounced until in March, 1922,
the price of food was 38.7 per cent above its 1913 average
as compared with the 66.9 per cent above its 1913 average
shown by the cost of living.[1] Obviously the fluctuations in
the food index since about 1916 have been unrepresentative
of changes in the cost of living, first because they rose too
rapidly, and subsequently because they fell too rapidly; and

[1] *Monthly Labor Review,* February, 1924, p. 94 [310].

so the changes in the Corporation's common labor rate must be compared with the more representative index of the cost of living available for the last half of its period of operations. This comparison, however, will have to be made on a 1913 base because there is no possibility of shifting the Bureau's index of the cost of living to the earlier period 1901-1905; the data were not collected for that period. The foregoing comparison brings out clearly an important fact obscured by the preceding method, viz., that the drastic wage cut in August, 1921, was much greater than the fall in living costs justified. Moreover, this disparity continued to exist for an entire year, that is, until the advance of wages in September, 1922.

But it must be remembered that these sets of relative numbers have presented facts in relation to a common starting point that has been taken as " 100 ". In other words, the average wage for 1901-1905 and the average price of food for the same period have each been called " 100 " in the first comparison; the wage rate for 1913 and the cost of living in the same year have each been equated to " 100 " in the second. In neither case has it been assumed that the wage rates secured to their receivers a " real " income above, equal to, or below some standard of living, but when wages and cost of living are both referred to an average or a rate designated as " 100 ", it is a little difficult to remember that there is nothing implied concerning the equality or inequality of these " 100's ". The question arises, then, what is the relation between these starting points, or, more precisely, what can be shown about the purchasing power of the annual earnings of day labor in Corporation plants? The significance of this is obvious, for if average annual earnings for 1901-1905 or 1913 were just sufficient to meet minimum subsistence needs in these base periods, then our relative figures carry quite a different story from that under the condition that the average annual earnings were twice the subsistence level.

But "subsistence level" raises another question: subsistence for the laborer only, or for his family; and if for a family, what size family? Obviously not subsistence for the laborer alone, for there can be no question of the social undesirability of setting such a low standard as that; but on the size of the family there may be more dispute. It has been customary to estimate budgets on the basis of the needs of a family of five despite the claims occasionally advanced by employers in wage arbitration cases that their employees' families averaged less than three children. These claims find considerable support in the conclusion of Miss M. L. Stecker that:

> The family of five where the father is the only wage-earner and all children are under 14 years of age, which has been selected as the normal or typical family, is apparently not most representative of American wage-earners, since in families where the father is the only wage-earner and all children are under 14 years of age the average size is smaller than this, while in families having five members there is an average of more than one wage-earner.[1]

The first part of this conclusion, viz., that in cases where all children are under 14 and the father the sole wage-earner the average family is less than five, is the more important here. For this Miss Stecker relies upon the data collected in the 1901 investigation of the United States Bureau of Labor. As she states elsewhere, a "study of available data . . . indicates how confused is the evidence on the validity of this family [five] as the standard unit."[2]   The contention might

[1] Stecker, M. L., "Family Budgets and Wages", *The American Economic Review*, vol. xi, p. 465. (September, 1921.)

[2] *Ibid.*, p. 458.

be made that her conclusion is based on too slender a foundation, but data collected by Professor Douglas in a paper recently published go far toward remedying that defect.[1] However, that is not the issue to which it is here desired to draw attention. As Professor Ogburn has pointed out,

The theory back of the selection of three children as a standard average is, however, more or less irrelevant, except, of course, in broad limits, of the actual number of children in a family, in very much the same way that the standard minimum-of-subsistence wage is more or less irrelevant to the actual wage received. Public sentiment has, however, supported the family-of-five standard, since in order that the race may maintain itself two children must grow to maturity, marry, and in turn bear children. Three children are simply a recognition of the undoubted chance of death, of non-marriage, and of infertility.[2]

Subsequently Professor Ogburn takes up the more or less current opinion " that any wage which workers work for is a living wage, since in order to work they must be alive." To this he replies: " The answer is that workers trying to live on less than a living wage do not live on it." [3] In support of his contention he cites such evidence as the infant death rate studies of the Children's Bureau of the United States Department of Labor. Aggregate figures from Brockton and New Bedford, Massachusetts, Manchester, New Hampshire, and Saginaw, Michigan, collected in 1912 and 1913, were summarized by the Bureau as follows: For families in which the father received less than $550 a year the infant mortality rate was 167; for families in which the

[1] Douglas, P. H., "Is the Family of Five Typical?" *The Journal of the American Statistical Association*, vol. xix, pp. 314-328 (September, 1924.)

[2] Ogburn, W. F., " The Standard-of-Living Factor in Wages," *Papers and Proceedings of the Thirty-fifth Annual Meeting of the American Economic Association*, March, 1923, pp. 121-122.

[3] *Ibid.*, p. 126.

income was between $550 and $649 the rate was 127.7; but
for families in which the father received $1,050 and over the
rate was only 53.4.[1]

In other words, the main justification for demanding that
wages be adequate to support a family of five is found in
social policy. Moreover, the evidence cited at least suggests
that one reason why there are not more families in which
the father is the sole bread-winner and in which there are
three children under 14, is that the children have not lived
to be enumerated.

Other objections to the whole conception of a minimum
standard are discussed by Miss Stecker and Professor Ogburn. Both agree that more work needs to be done in devising tools and measurements which will make the use of
the concept more accurate and more objective. With this
the present writer is in accord, but in an historical study it
is obviously necessary to use the tools, crude though they
may be, that were worked out contemporaneously. It is
impossible at this date to compute accurately a subsistence
budget for the Pittsburgh or Chicago steel districts for all
the years since 1901. Consequently, the following section
will compare available budgets and estimates with annual
earnings.

In attempting to secure some idea of these annual earnings the possibility remains of making the absurd assumption that the employee on the common labor rate worked
twelve hours a day for 365 days in the year. Then in 1901,
the first year the Corporation operated, the absolute maximum for common labor was $657.00. For this year the U. S.
Bureau of Labor made an exhaustive survey of living costs
as revealed in workingmen's family budgets. No attempt
was made to estimate a " minimum " budget, but in Bulletin

[1] U. S. Children's Bureau, Bulletin No. 37, *Infant Mortality, Results
of a Field Study in Brockton, Mass.*, p. 32.

54 (p. 1146) of the U. S. Bureau of Labor a summary table of some of the data in the larger study permits one interesting comparison. The table presents the "Average expenditure per family for various purposes in 1901". For the North Atlantic states, 13,782 families reporting, the items total $1081.41. This includes such duplications as rent for the eighty-seven per cent who paid it and payments on mortgages for others who were buying homes. Moreover, several items were paid by only a small percentage of the families. The elimination of the duplications and the unrepresentative items reduces the total to $815.14, a figure far above the maximum possible earnings of the Corporation's common laborer, and still farther above what he actually made. Such a comparison is not as significant as others to follow, but at this date it seems impossible to compute a "minimum" budget from the 1901 data.

For about five years subsequent to the Bureau of Labor's study there seems to have been little or no work done on budgets, but in the years 1906 to 1910 inclusive this deficiency was remedied. Of the more important studies the first in point of the period covered was that of Mrs. Louise B. More, *Wage-Earners' Budgets; a study of standards and cost of living in New York City.* The work consisted of an analysis of the budgets of 200 families who were ". . . able and willing to co-operate with the investigator intelligently and patiently in *keeping simple accounts* and in making careful, verifiable statements." One of the conclusions reached was that

. . . a " fair living wage " for a workingman's family of average size in New York City should be at least $728 a year, or a steady income of $14 a week. Making allowances for a larger proportion of surplus than was found in these families [average surplus $15.13 a year], which is necessary to provide adequately for the future, the income should be somewhat larger than this—that is, from $800 to $900 a year.[1]

On the impossible schedule of 365 twelve-hour days a laborer might have earned $678.90 in 1906. Since the average wage for all employees was only $50 more than this, it is certain that he earned nothing like this maximum.

For 1907 Professor R. C. Chapin's *Standard of Living Among Workingmen's Families in New York City* is available. Based upon 391 families and representing the most painstaking care, it has long been considered a classic piece of work. The most important facts for this study are contained in the following extract.

It seems safe to conclude from all the data that we have been considering that an income under $800 is not enough to permit the maintenance of a normal standard. A survey of the detail of expenditure for each item in the budget shows some manifest deficiency for almost every family in the $600 and $700 groups.

Among the deficiencies brought out are those in food, clothing, and house space. In the income group $600 to $799 Chapin found 32 per cent underfed, 57 per cent underclothed, and 58 per cent overcrowded.[2] The Corporation's common laborer on maximum hours might have earned $722.70 in 1907.[3]

[1] Quoted in the Bureau of Applied Economics, *Standards of Living* (Bulletin Number 7, Washington, 1920), pp. 149, 150.

[2] Chapin, R. C., *Standard of Living Among Workingmen's Families in New York City* (New York, 1909), p. 245.

[3] It will probably be objected that comparisons should not be made between wages earned in the Pittsburgh and Chicago districts and living costs in New York City. But the differences between living costs in New York City and the Pittsburgh steel district during 1906 to 1909 at least have been demonstrated to be negligible. Mrs. More's study showed a steady income of at least $14 a week necessary in New York City; Professor Chapin's figure was $800 a year. The next budget presented

The next accurate budgetary study available covers the period from October 1, 1907, to April 1, 1908. It is particularly valuable because it was made in the " Pittsburgh district ". Between the dates mentioned Miss Margaret Byington, an investigator for the Pittsburgh Survey, secured the cooperation of a number of families in Homestead, Pennsylvania, in keeping budgets of weekly expenditures. A study of these budgets, comparisons with the prices of commodities, and intimate contact over the six months with the households which supplied them convinced Miss Byington that

only when earnings are $15 a week, or more, can we confidently look for a reasonable margin above the requisite expenditures for necessities. It is only in the group spending more than $20 that we find that the average family has reached a point where, without being spendthrift of the future and without undue pinching in other directions, they can spend enough to satisfy what we should recognize as the reasonable ambitions of an American who puts his life into his work.[1]

She found that a large number of the foreign unskilled workmen were making only $9.90 a week; that is, they

in the text is for Homestead, Pennsylvania, for part of the same period as is covered in Professor Chapin's work and shows a steady income of $15 a week to be necessary there. This means $780 a year, almost precisely Professor Chapin's figure. More conclusive than the foregoing, however, is the report of the British Board of Trade on *The Cost of Living in American Towns.* The conclusions of the report were based on a study of rents and retail prices of food in 28 cities. The data collected convinced the investigators that on the basis of the criteria stated living costs in New York and Pittsburgh in 1909 were identical (p. 356 of the edition of the study published in this country as Sen. Doc. 22, 62nd Congress, 1st session). As will appear later the budgets used for more recent years are more generalized so that the error involved in comparing them with wages in the Pittsburgh and Chicago districts is not great.

[1] Byington, M. F., *Homestead: the Households of a Mill Town* (New York, 1910), pp. 105-106. At least two-thirds of this book is devoted to an analysis of the budgets mentioned above.

were working six ten-hour days at .165 an hour. If we again make the assumption of maximum work, we find that seven days of twelve hours each bring $13.86, still below the figure set by Miss Byington as necessary to secure any margin above necessities. Unemployment of even the shortest duration would, of course, aggravate the situation.

At about the time of Miss Byington's work, though extending over a longer period, the Immigration Commission was making an exhaustive study that covered part of the same ground. In the Pittsburgh district it was found that the foreign-born heads of families employed in the iron and steel industry earned an annual average of $413, and that 50.1 per cent of this group earned less than $400 a year.[1] These foreign-born workmen were, in large part, receiving the common labor rate. The investigation was not confined to Corporation plants and something must be added to these figures because of the fact that the Corporation usually paid higher wages to common labor than its competitors; but even so this figure would be little more than half the $780 Miss Byington's estimate would be on a yearly basis[2]

A budget obviously valuable for such a study as this was prepared in 1910 by the Associated Charities of Pittsburgh. Their work was based on that of W. O. Atwater of the United States Department of Agriculture for quantities of food necessary to maintain in health and efficiency a family of five: father, mother, boy of 13, girl of

[1] Reports of the Immigration Commission: *Immigrants in Industries,* part 2: *Iron and Steel Manufacturing* (Washington, 1911), vol. i, pp. 61, 62. (Senate Document 633 of the 61st Cong. 2nd sess.).

[2] In the face of these facts the estimate of the Pittsburgh Chamber of Commerce on the cost of food alone for a family of five in Pittsburgh in 1909, the common labor rate in Corporation plants still being .165, is nothing short of ludicrous. The figure set by this worthy body was $11.88; indeed a poor prospect for the laborer whose pay for seven days of twelve hours was $13.86!

11, and girl of 9. Other items were secured largely from budgetary studies of workmen's families in Pittsburgh. The final result was characterized as " a sum that the father of three children . . . must spend on the dire necessities of life ". The items were as follows:

Food	$382.00	Tobacco	$ 5.20
Clothing	151.00	Recreation	13.00
Fuel	25.00	Medicine	18.50
Light	6.25	Sundries &	
Rent	120.00	Incidentals	39.00
Insurance	18.20		
		Total	$778.15 [1]

The average common labor rate in Corporation mills during 1910 was .1716 (.165 from January 1 to May 1 and .175 thereafter). Thus at twelve hours a day for 365 days the laborer would get $751.61 or $26.54 less than the estimated minimum of subsistence. Moreover, it should be noted that in 1911 the cost of living remained practically constant with that of 1910, and in 1912 advanced sharply; but that for both those years the common labor rate remained at .175. A total of 365 days of twelve hours each at this rate would amount to $766.50, still below the Associated Charities' minimum. Thus for these three years common laborers in Corporation mills were facing the physical impossibility of earning a wage adequate to support a family of five. The result, according to the Charities' report, was that people in this wage group were not living. " They were slowly but surely starving. That is the simple truth which was painfully brought to our attention." [2]

The Charity Organization Society of Chicago also made a study of living costs in 1910 for " an unskilled laborer,

---

[1] *Stanley Hearings*, 1911, vol. iv, p. 2957. The items are given as in the text, but the total was erroneously recorded as $768, or $10 too low, and was rather widely quoted at the time.

[2] *Ibid.*, p. 2956.

wife, and three children living in South Chicago ". The items were as follows:

Rent	$108.00	Clothing	
Food, $6 a week ...	312.00	For man	$ 28.00
1½ qts. milk daily ..	43.68	For woman	10.00
Light & fuel	50.00	For children	24.00
		For shoes	38.00
		Insurance	15.80
		Total	$629.48 [1]

It will be noticed that there is no allowance made for sickness, utensils, the numerous petty incidentals that always arise, tobacco, reading matter, or any recreation of any sort. The budget is unquestionably too meagre; but as it stands, since the common labor rate in Chicago was the same as that in Pittsburgh, the maximum number of hours a year would mean a total of $122.13 above this budget in 1910 and $135.02 above in 1911 and 1912.

So far the computations have been made for wages on the preposterous assumption that the laborer could get employment for twelve hours each of the 365 days of 1910, but it will be recalled that 1910 is the one year for which it is possible to make a definite statement on the number of hours a common laborer might expect to work a year.[2] Briefly stated we found that he could not hope for more than 45 weeks' work and that common labor averaged 72 hours a week in 1910. At .1716 an hour the year's earnings were $556. This figure is $222 below the minimum set by the Pittsburgh Charities, and $74 below that set by the Chicago Charities.

The next year for which a satisfactory minimum family budget has been found is 1914: the estimate of the New York State Factory Investigation Commission. The detailed figures follow:

[1] *Stanley Hearings*, 1911, vol. iv, p. 2993.

[2] See pp. 62, 63, *supra*.

Food	$325.00	Carfare	$ 31.20
Rent	200.00	Health	22.00
Fuel & light	20.00	Education,	
Clothing	140.00	newspaper	5.63
Insurance		Recreation &	
Man	20.00	amusement	50.00
Family	15.60	Miscellaneous	40.00
Furnishings	7.00		
		Total	$876.43 [1]

The hourly rate paid to common laborers in 1914 was .20.
Our hypothetical worker who put in maximum hours every
day in the year would receive exactly $876. Since 1914 was
a bad year for the Corporation, employees in the manufacturing subsidiaries being about 34,000 less than in 1913, it
is certain that actual earnings were a great deal less than
this hypothetical figure.

For 1918 the minimum budget prepared by Professor W.
F. Ogburn of Columbia University is undoubtedly the best
available. It is based on 600 actual budgets of shipyard
workers in the New York ship-building area and, with the
possible exception of the item for street car fare, seems applicable to steel workers in the Pittsburgh district. The
items are supposed to provide a minimum of health and
decency for a family of five for a year:

Food	$615	Street-car fare	$ 40
Clothing		Paper, books, etc.	9
Man	76	Amusements, drinks,	
Woman	55	and tobacco	50
11 to 14 years	40	Sickness	60
7 to 10 years	33	Dentist, occulist,	
4 to 6 years	30	glasses, etc.	3
Rent	180	Furnishings	35
Fuel and light	62	Laundry	4
Insurance	40	Cleaning supplies	15
Organizations	12	Miscellaneous	20
Religion	7		
		Total	$1,386 [2]

[1] Interchurch, *Report on the Steel Strike of 1919*, p. 258.
[2] *Ibid.*, p. 257.

It will be remembered that by March, 1918, the wage index was definitely above the food index. The average common labor rate for 1918 was .3961. This multiplied by our hypothetical maximum hours would give $1734.92 for the year, a figure well above Professor Ogburn's minimum. But the average annual wage of " all employees " including the highest paid officials was only $1685, an amount $50 below the maximum possible figure for common labor just computed. On the more rational assumption of 45 weeks' work of 72 hours each, the laborer would have earned in 1918 only $1296, exactly $90 below Professor Ogburn's minimum. Since the absurdity of a situation in which common labor gets $50 a year more than the average wage of all employees requires no comment, it can be safely said that the second figure is nearer the truth than the first.

But nothing more can be safely said: $1296 is *nearer* the truth than $1734. Just as we found that the Corporation actually knew how many men worked on the twelve-hour shift for only four months of the twenty-three years of its history, so we find now that it knows even less about the number of men receiving the common labor rate. After all, the preceding pages are meaningless if only one-tenth of one per cent are paid the common labor rate. The Corporation rather prides itself on the publicity which it gives its own affairs, and in many respects its annual reports certainly support this position, but on this item there are only two statements. Judge Gary testified to the Senate Committee investigating the steel strike of 1919 that 46,638 or 24.4 per cent of the employees in the manufacturing companies were receiving the common labor rate at that time.[1] In a letter to the Interchurch Commission of Inquiry Judge Gary stated that 70,000 men received that rate,[2] but there is noth-

[1] *Senate Hearings*, 1919, p. 199.
[2] Interchurch, *Report on the Steel Strike of 1919*, p. 5.

ing in the *Report* to indicate whether these 70,000 were manufacturing or other employees or to indicate the date on which the statement was true. A request directed to the Corporation for additional light on this statement in the Interchurch *Report* was never answered.

In view of the fact that in 1910 49.69 per cent of the 172,706 workers covered received the common labor rate, and that the development of the industry had been tending for years prior to 1910 to reduce the percentage on this rate,[1] it is certain that a larger proportion than Judge Gary's 24.4 per cent have, at some time, worked for this lowest rate. In a conversation in his office the Comptroller of the Corporation told the writer that it would be impossible to find out for the entire Corporation the number of men on that rate over any period of time, since the data were scattered from Chicago to Birmingham and could not be collected without unwarranted expense. They have apparently been compiled only once: under the pressure of the Senate investigation. Consequently, it is impossible to get nearer to the truth than to say that from 25 to 50 or more per cent of the Corporation's manufacturing employees have received the common labor rate at various times, and that the percentage has tended downward.

Because of the dearth of data the immediately preceding discussion has necessarily been more or less of a patched together affair, particularly unsatisfactory from the point of view of continuity. Moreover, the assumption most frequently made concerning wages; that is, that a laborer might work 365 days of twelve hours each, is so far beyond the bounds of reason that it is difficult to make the proper allowances and the reader is likely to form a conception of the relation of wages to living costs that is not justified by the facts. Consequently, it has seemed advisable to make a

[1] Neill, *op. cit.,* vol. i, p. xxxii, and vol. iii, p. 81.

comparison which is not only of a more continuous nature
but which is believed to be a closer approximation of the
facts. It must be noted that it is avowedly an approximation only, but, as will be seen, the relations brought out are
for most years of such a nature as to justify conclusions as
to whether wages were above or below living costs, though
not to justify statements as to the degree of difference between the two levels. In making the comparisons the rates
per hour for common labor furnished by the Corporation
have been multiplied by 3240 hours a year to secure figures
for annual wages. 3240 hours represent 45 weeks' employment at 72 hours a week, the figures true for 1910. To the
extent that the Corporation has reduced excessive schedules,
72 hours a week is too high for years subsequent to 1910,
but the error is in the Corporation's favor since it forces
the wage figure higher. Moreover, 72 hours is fifty per cent
above the 48 hours that are more and more widely being
accepted as the standard work week. That 45 weeks a year
was all the average employee on the common labor rate could
expect to get during the first eleven years of the Corporation's history is strongly indicated in the *Report on Conditions of Employment in the Iron and Steel Industry in the
United States.*[1] The evidence submitted there, summarized

[1] The seventh chapter of volume three of Neill's report is devoted to
"Irregularity of Employment". The following points in the chapter
are particularly significant. ". . . there was no complaint so frequently made or so strongly expressed [by the workmen] as that regarding irregularity of employment." (p. 205) "In 1909 the steel
works and rolling mills had relatively the largest fluctuation in the
size of the labor force of any of the large manufacturing industries."
(p. 205, footnote). This statement is made on the basis of the data
secured in the census of manufactures for 1909. Those data and additional figures for 1904, 1914, and 1919 are included to show that the
situation had existed prior to the Bureau of Labor's investigation and
has continued to exist subsequently.

in the footnote below, was gathered from both Corporation

Industry	Per cent which minimum number of employees was of maximum			
	1904	1909	1914	1919
Iron and steel, steel works and rolling mills.	61.4	75.8	77.4	66.2
Foundry and machine shop products......	64.4	80.7	85.6	85.6
Lumber and timber products	57.3	87.8	83.0	78.0
Cars and general shop construction and repairs by steam railroad companies.....	76.8	89.1	95.4	91.0
Woolen, worsted, felt goods and wool hats.	70.8	91.0	89.9	60.4
Tobacco, cigars, cigarettes	70.2	91.6	95.9	74.3
Clothing and shirts, men's.............	73.9	91.8	88.2	73.1
Boots and shoes	71.5	91.8	90.2	87.1
Printing and publishing................	75.5	93.3	95.9	90.5
Cotton goods.........................	81.1	97.6	94.7	92.4

It will be noted that "iron and steel" had the greatest fluctuation in 1909 and 1914 but was second to "lumber and timber products" in 1904 and second to "woolen and worsted, felt goods and wool hats" in 1919. (*Census of Manufactures*, 1905, part i [covering the year 1904], p. 26 *et. seq.; Abstract of Statistics of Manufacturing*, 1909, p. 22 *et. seq.; Abstract of Statistics of Manufacturing*, 1914, p. 466 *et seq.; Abstract of Statistics of Manufacturing*, 1919, p. 21 *et seq.*)

A table is presented on page 208 of Neill's third volume showing the "approximate average number of men employed in blast furnaces, each month, 1907 to 1911." The range was "from 18,545 in January, 1908, to 46,810 in February, 1910." The report continues: "In 31 of the 60 months these fluctuations amounted to 1,000 or more employees, and in several other cases they were only 100 short of that number. In more than one-half of the months from 1907 to 1911, inclusive, therefore, 1,000 men were being taken on or discharged from the labor force for the blast furnaces alone." (p. 209). "Considering the iron and steel industry as a whole the fluctuations in employment were much greater than is indicated by the figures for the blast furnaces alone." (p. 210). This statement is substantiated by a table on pages 210 and 211 showing the fluctuations by months from January, 1905, to December, 1910, in a large plant which had ".... a reputation throughout the industry of being one of the most constant in its operation and of suffering less from periods of depression than most of the large steel plants." (p. 210). For the year 1910 alone the Bureau of Labor found that of the 90,757 employees for whom it could tabulate the records only 37.6 per cent could get employment "48 weeks and over." (p. 213).

and independent plants. The only data for the Corporation alone are unsatisfactory because they cover less than half of the Corporation's history, 1915 to 1923 inclusive, and because they include all employees. Since the clerical and executive employees probably remain at a fairly constant figure, their inclusion tends to obscure the fluctuations in the numbers of *bona fide* steel makers. Moreover, the years included would hardly be considered " normal " under any definition of that term, but since these figures are the only ones available they are presented for what they are worth.

TABLE IX

FLUCTUATIONS IN TOTAL EMPLOYEES, U. S. STEEL CORPORATION
1915-1923 [1]

Year	Maximum Employees (average) in any Month	Minimum Employees (average) in any Month	Per cent which Minimum is of Maximum
1915	227,051 (Dec.)	141,461 (Jan.)	62.3
1916	265,919	232,540	87.4
1917	277,526	250,836	90.3
1918	283,414 (July)	241,490 (Jan.)	85.2
1919	274,837 (Feb.)	213,081 (Oct.)	77.5
1920	275,552 (Mar.)	261,037 (May)	94.7
1921	263,308 (Jan.)	157,083 (July)	59.6
1922	253,360 (Nov.)	186,542 (Feb.)	73.6
1923	277,779 (Oct.)	240,586 (Feb.)	86.6

A continuous series of estimates of the minimum cost of sustaining a family of five in health and decency was secured from Professor Ogburn's 1918 figures as a starting place. This budget was computed on the prices of June, 1918, at which time the Bureau of Labor's index of food prices stood at 165 on 1913 prices as 100. Reference to the table on page 67 will remind the reader that in the years

[1] Compiled from annual reports of the Corporation.

1914 to 1918 inclusive the Bureau of Labor had collected data for a general cost-of-living index including food, clothing, housing, and other items for the month of December only. Consequently, for years prior to 1919 the only practical method of converting Professor Ogburn's 1918 budget into a figure approximately true for those years is to multiply his total of $1386 by the index of food prices; that is, if $1386 is the figure for June 1918, when the food index stood at 165, then the total budget for 1913 was $840. ($840 : $1386 :: 100 · 165). As stated, this seems to be the only practical way to secure a continuous series of estimates of a minimum budget. The merit of using Professor Ogburn's budget in preference to some others is that it has been more widely accepted than any other and can be relied upon as done with the utmost care. However, it is very interesting to note that the results are almost exactly the same as those which would be secured by the use of the 1910 budget of the Pittsburgh Associated Charities. Their budget, it will be recalled, was $778. If Professor Ogburn's $1386 for 1918 is reduced to a 1910 basis by the use of th food index it will be found equivalent to a budget of $775.62. For 1919 and subsequent years the estimates of minimum needs for a family of five are based on the Bureau of Labor's index of changes in the cost of living. Since setting a minimum cost of living at some precise number of dollars gives an impression of accuracy that is not warranted, the following table shows the estimated cost for each year as falling within limits of $50. The actual figure reached by the computations just described is near the mid-point between the designated limits. With these data are combined the annual earnings received by a common laborer who worked 72 hours a week for 45 weeks. As stated before, the figures in the column " deficit or surplus " in the table below must not be interpreted to mean that in any year the figure shows

TABLE X

COMPARISON OF ESTIMATED ANNUAL EARNINGS OF COMMON LABORERS
WITH THE COST OF LIVING FOR A FAMILY OF FIVE 1901-1922

Year	Annual Earnings at Common Labor Rate (estimated)	Cost of Living for a family of five	Deficit or Surplus
1901	$486	$575 to $625	—$89 to —$139
1902	505	600 to 650	— 95 to — 145
1903	518	600 to 650	— 82 to — 132
1904	470	625 to 675	—155 to — 205
1905	494	625 to 675	—131 to — 181
1906	502	650 to 700	—148 to — 198
1907	535	675 to 725	—140 to — 190
1908	535	675 to 725	—140 to — 190
1909	535	725 to 775	—190 to — 240
1910	556	750 to 800	—194 to — 244
1911	567	750 to 800	—183 to — 233
1912	567	800 to 850	—233 to — 283
1913	641	825 to 875	—181 to — 231
1914	648	825 to 875	—173 to — 223
1915	648	825 to 875	—173 to — 223
1916	776	925 to 975	—149 to — 199
1917	969	1200 to 1250	—231 to — 281
1918	1296	1375 to 1425	— 79 to — 129
1919	1637	1550 to 1600	+ 87 to + 37
1920	1724	1725 to 1775	— 1 to — 51
1921	1343	1475 to 1525	—132 to — 182
1922	1037	1375 to 1425	—238 to — 288
1923	....	1400 to 1450	

the actual difference between probable earnings and cost of
living for a family of five. However, it is significant that
in the years 1901 to 1918 inclusive the best year's figures indicate a deficit of a little more than $75, and that for fourteen
of these eighteen years the probable deficit ranged from a
minimum of about $125 to a maximum of about $275. With
the possible exception of 1918 it is highly improbable that
errors sufficient to produce such large minimum divergencies
are contained in the two sets of estimates. Consequently,
though no attempt is made here to prove the extent to which
earnings fell below living costs, it is definitely affirmed that

the above table shows that for the first seventeen or eighteen years of its operation the Corporation did not pay to the average common laborer in its employ sufficient wages to enable him to support a normal size family in health and decency. Such a conclusion receives considerable support from the fact that cigar factories and similar " complementary " industries in which woman and child labor can be utilized flourish in steel districts, and from the further fact that a large proportion of families in which the man is a common laborer take lodgers.[1]

So far attention has been concentrated on the unskilled labor groups. What sort of wages are received by skilled and semiskilled men and what percentage do they form of the total? When the *Report on Conditions of Employment in the Iron and Steel Industry in the United States* was made in 1910 the skilled groups received $0.25 an hour and up, and constituted 23.6 per cent of the total; the semiskilled received $0.18 and under $0.25 an hour, and were 26.71 per cent of the total. These wage rates are applicable to Corporation plants, but the percentages may or may not be. The Comptroller states that the Corporation has never attempted to classify its employees in this fashion. Moreover, the various investigations have developed no data applicable to the Corporation alone covering either a large enough number of occupations or a long enough period of time to be significant for this study. In the 1919 hearing, for example, Mr. Gary stated that the " highest earnings " of mill employees went to the " rollers, $32.56 a day ".[2] Further questions developed the fact that one man of the more than a quarter of a million employed received this wage.[3] Mr.

---

[1] *Cf.* Byington, *op. cit.,* pp. 143, 201 ; *Reports of the Immigration Commission, op. cit.,* part 2, vol. i, pp. 70-84 ; Neill, *op. cit.,* vol. iii, p. 214.

[2] *Senate Hearings,* 1919, p. 156.

[3] *Ibid.,* p. 159.

Gary also gave the common labor rate, the general average wage for the manufacturing companies, and similar averages for the coal, coke, iron, shipbuilding, and transportation subsidiaries for certain months and years, usually 1914 and 1919. But in no place has the Corporation made available any detailed figures on wages above the common labor rate. Requests for such data brought the reply that it would cost too much to assemble them from the various subsidiaries. It would be possible to go through the latest bulletin of the Bureau of Labor Statistics on wages and hours in the steel industry, select the occupations above the common labor level, and reproduce here the facts there presented; but this has not been done for the reasons that it is a waste of space, and that the government figures are collected from the industry at large and can give only some general indication of the situation in Corporation mills. One assertion can be safely made: to a small percentage of highly skilled employees the Corporation pays excellent wages; to a larger group of less skilled men it pays good wages. More than this on rates cannot be said, but in addition to these higher wages some of the men received additional payments in the form of bonuses.

The bonus scheme, announced in December, 1902, has undergone considerable modifications of detail from time to time but its essential features have remained about the same. Certain sums are necessary in a given year to meet interest charges, make deposits on sinking funds, and pay the normal rate of dividends. If these items were more than provided for by the year's earnings, the Corporation set aside a certain percentage of the net earnings to be divided among the men occupying " official and semi-official positions and who are engaged in directing and managing the affairs of the Corporation and of its several subsidiary companies." The form in which the men received their bonuses has varied a great deal.   In one or two years it has been paid all in cash and in one lump sum; in others, part in cash and part in stock, payment of the cash being distributed over a year and of the stock over a longer period.   For the first year in which the plan operated, 1903, the details were as follows.

To meet the items of interest, sinking funds, and dividends in 1903, $75,000,000 were needed.   It was provided that if $80,000,000 and less than $90,000,000 were made, one per cent of net earnings should be set aside; if $90,000,000 and less than $100,000,000 were made, one and two-tenths per cent should be set aside; and so on until if $150,000,000 and less than $160,000,000 were made, two and five-tenths per cent should be set aside.   One-half of the amount thus reserved was to be paid in quarterly installments through 1904, the other half reserved until the end of 1904 and then invested in preferred stock of the Corporation.   The stock was to be divided and one-half given to the employees entitled to it, the remainder being held by the Corporation.   Certificates representing the individual's interests were to be issued to him, each certificate carrying, among others, the following provisions:

First.   That if he remains continuously in the service of the Corporation or of one or another of its subsidiary companies for five years, the stock shall be delivered to him and he may do as he likes with it.

Second.   That if he dies or becomes totally and permanently disabled while in the employ of the Corporation or of one or another of its subsidiary companies, the stock will be delivered to his estate or to him.

Third.   That he can draw the dividends declared on the stock while it is held for his account and he remains in the employ of the Corporation or of one or another of its subsidiary companies.

Fourth.   That if without previous consent voluntarily he

shall have quitted the service of the Corporation or of its subsidiary companies, he shall forfeit all right to this stock, and in such case it will be held in a fund which at the end of five years will be divided among such employees as shall have complied with all the conditions.

A year or two later provision was made that an employee lost his claim to this reserved stock if he was discharged. The men receiving the bonus were to be selected according to merit and the whole transaction was to be a private affair between employer and employee, no employee being supposed to know what bonus another employee received or even whether or not he received one.[1]

In the administration of the plan possibilities of repression are clear. By 1906 the certificate of interest in the

---

[1] The facts stated above were secured from Fitch, *The Steel Workers* (New York, 1911), pp. 309, 310, 320-324. These pages contain a memorandum on the bonus system supplied to Mr. Fitch from the office of Mr. Gary. The detailed facts are available only to 1910; since then the only information available has been a sentence or two in the annual report stating that extra compensation in accordance with the plan begun in 1903 has been paid. The annual reports for 1921, 1922 and 1923 contained no such statement, however. The first omission doubtless resulted in part from the fact that 1921 was a poor year but the following paragraph from the 1923 report throws additional light on the matter:
" Appropriation was made from the earnings for 1923 of a fund for distribution under and in accordance with the Profit Sharing Plan adopted by the stockholders in 1921. The allotment and distribution was made in February 1924 by the Profit Sharing Committee of stockholders elected at the annual stockholders' meeting in April 1923. Of the awards made by the Committee, one-half was paid in cash and the remainder covered by Certificates of Conditional Interest in shares of Common Stock of the Corporation in which the Committee invested such part of the appropriation. The stock covered by the certificates is deliverable to holders in January 1929, provided they are then in the service of the Corporation or its subsidiaries, or is deliverable prior to that date if they die while in the service or are retired under the Corporation's pension plan." (p. 30).
This "profit-sharing" plan appears to have been substituted for the bonus and to closely resemble the latter in administration, but a request for additional information was refused by the Corporation.

shares of stock held back for five years stipulated that during this five years the employee should have rendered "faithful and satisfactory service" as a condition of getting his stock. Moreover, it will be recalled that the cash payments were, with one or two exceptions, not given to the men when the profits were ascertained but were doled out quarterly during the entire year following that for which they were earned. If this plan is really nothing more than a profit-sharing scheme it seems unnecessary to complicate it in such a manner that any man who is regularly getting bonuses from year to year stands to lose a great deal if for any reason he quits or is discharged. Finally, the secret nature of the plan is extraordinary and, as a matter of fact, seems quite unnecessary.

A final bit of comparison is in the following table showing total receipts, wages and salaries, and "profits", in each year of the Corporation's operations from 1902 to 1923.[1] The most interesting aspect of the figures is the change in the relative parts of the total receipts going to wages and salaries and to profits. In the earlier years the

[1] Figures for 1901 are not available. "Profits" as used in the table is the aggregate of dividends, annual surplus, interest on bonds of the Corporation, interest on the bonds, mortgages, and purchase money obligations of the subsidiary companies, and inter-company profit reserves. In some years, such as 1921, there was neither an annual surplus nor an inter-company profit reserve, in others only one of them appears. In such a case the "profits" item represents the sum of the dividends and interest payments less the amount withdrawn from the surplus account, or less the "net balance of profits earned by subsidiary companies on sales made and service rendered account of materials which were on hand at first of year in purchasing companies' inventories and which profits were realized in cash during the year from the standpoint of a combined statement of the business of all companies," or less the sum of these last two items. In other words, the Corporation deducts from its statement of net earnings in good years the inter-company profit reserve. I have restored it in these good years since it really is a part of profits. In bad years, however, when there is no inter-company profit reserve, consistency requires that the item which takes its place should be deducted. The same logic applies to the treatment of surplus.

percentages received were much nearer equal. In 1902, for example, the profits were equal to ninety-two per cent of the wages and salaries. The business situation in 1903 and 1904 reduced the percentage of profits but in the next three years equality was again fairly closely approached. From here until about 1918 business conditions were reflected rather definitely, particularly the bad year 1914, in which profits were only seven and five-tenths per cent of total receipts as compared with a percentage of twenty-eight and eight-tenths for wages and salaries, and the good year, 1916, in which profits got twenty-five and seven-tenths per cent of the total receipts and wages and salaries only twenty-one and two-tenths. War taxes cut very heavily into profits beginning in 1917, and in 1921 the business depression reduced profits to the smallest proportion of total receipts they have ever been. 1923 was for the steel industry a very good year, but even then profits constituted not quite ten per cent of total earnings as compared with twenty-nine and five-tenths per cent that went to wages and salaries. It is too soon to make any positive statements and the situation is complicated by the imposition and subsequent removal of a heavy burden of war taxes plus a serious depression, but with allowances made for all these factors the indications are that the relation between the proportions of total receipts going to profits on the one hand, and wages and salaries on the other has been altered to the gain of the latter group. In concluding his chapter on "The Division of the Product" in *Profits, Wages, and Prices,* Professor Friday observed that "Practically, the most difficult problem which labor has before it for the next decade is to hold this relative advantage which it has gained " [1] (during the war). Since it is impossible to separate wages from salaries in the Corporation's accounts it is also impossible to pass judgment as to

[1] P. 132.

whether its " labor ", as distinguished from hired managers
and executives, has held what it gained. Common labor
definitely lost in August, 1921, what it had gained, but
apparently regained at least part of the loss in September,
1922. Further than this one can only speculate.

TABLE XI

TOTAL RECEIPTS, WAGES, SALARIES AND PROFITS OF THE U. S. STEEL
CORPORATION, 1902-1923 [1]

Year	Total Receipts all Sources	Wages and Salaries	Profits	Per cent of total receipts of	
				Wages and Salaries	Profits
1902....	$569,065,902	$120,528,343	111,607,959	21.2	19.6
1903....	541,841,465	120,763,896	81,053,310	22.3	14.9
1904....	448,162,380	99,778,276	59,104,633	22.3	13.2
1905....	591,388,870	128,052,955	105,300,747	21.7	17.8
1906....	705,916,790	147,765,540	131,127,320	20.9	18.6
1907....	766,763,718	160,825,822	144,750,302	21.0	18.9
1908....	488,094,725	120,510,829	78,437,439	24.7	16.1
1909....	653,200,250	151,663,394	114,776,119	23.2	17.6
1910....	709,814,593	174,955,139	122,286,030	24.7	17.2
1911....	618,911,430	161,419,031	77,415,003	26.1	12.5
1912....	751,851,867	189,351,602	82,152,607	25.1	10.9
1913....	801,246,939	207,206,176	121,546,008	25.8	15.2
1914....	562,275,601	162,379,907	42,432,515	28.8	7.5
1915....	733,660,606	176,800,864	120,850,933	24.0	16.5
1916....	1,242,638,386	263,385,502	319,828,731	21.2	25.7
1917....	1,712,510,996	347,370,400	269,713,693	20.0	15.7
1918....	1,784,786,987	452,663,524	169,289,966	25.3	9.5
1919....	1,480,450,636	479,548,040	119,064,376	32.4	8.0
1920....	1,756,728,174	581,556,925	148,667,726	33.1	8.5
1921....	1,003,164,795	332,887,505	55,667,894	33.2	5.5
1922....	1,110,543,676	322,678,130	69,200,085	29.0	6.2
1923....	1,591,381,927	469,502,634	158,578,285	29.5	9.9
Total ...	20,623,400,713	5,371,594,434	2,702,851,681	....	....
Average.	937,427,305	244,163,338	122,856,894	26.0	13.1

[1]In the preparation of this table the writer was materially aided by the
*Report on Analysis of Earnings and Disposition thereof United States
Steel Corporation* which was prepared for the Director General of
Railroads by W. E. Lowe and J. L. Dohr, and by suggestions from
Mr. Dohr.

CHAPTER III

ATTITUDE OF CORPORATION TOWARD LABOR ORGANIZATIONS

Second only in importance to the question of wages is the attitude of the Corporation toward trade unions. However widely opinions may vary on the value of workmen's organizations to themselves and to society at large, there can be no argument on these statements of fact:

1. In spite of relapses in periods of depression the membership of such organizations has formed an increasingly larger proportion of " persons gainfully employed " with the passage of years.

2. The more industrialized a country becomes the greater economic and political significance these organizations attain.

These being facts, the attitude of the most powerful business organization in the world toward this development takes on added importance.

The official attitude of the Corporation at present can not be better shown than by quoting the following remarks of Mr. Gary at the annual meeting of the stockholders April 18, 1921.

As stated and repeated publicly, we do not combat, though we do not contract or deal with, labor unions as such. Personally, I believe they may have been justified in the long past, for I think the workmen were not always treated justly; that because of their lack of experience or otherwise they were unable to protect themselves; and therefore needed the assistance of outsiders in order to secure their rights.

But whatever may have been the conditions of employment in the long past, and whatever may have been the results of unionism, concerning which there is at least much uncertainty, there is at present, in the opinion of the large majority of both employers and employes, no necessity for labor unions; and that no benefit or advantage through them will accrue to any-one except the union labor leaders.[1]

Though this particular sentence is quoted from an address of 1921, it had been " repeated," as Mr. Gary says, on many preceding occasions. Its meaning is clear enough. The Corporation admits that it does not approve of unions. They are in its eyes outworn relics of a preceding age. But it contends that it does " not combat labor unions as such."

Now let us turn to the record and see how the Corporation reached this position and whether or not it actually has combated unions " as such." It is not my purpose to pre-sent a history of trade unionism in the steel industry, but the following facts seem to be essential to a comprehension of the development of the Corporation's policy.

As far back as 1858 the Sons of Vulcan, made up of puddlers and their helpers, were secretly organized.[2] During the sixties a number of independent and local unions devel-oped among the heaters and roll hands. These unions did not admit the lower paid men of the rolling crews, and so about 1870 another union designated as the " Iron and Steel Roll Hands of the United States " was formed. In 1873 steps were taken to unite these three groups, the second hav-ing by that time solidified into the Associated Brotherhood of Iron and Steel Heaters, Rollers, and Roughers. At that time they had a total of 700 members in twenty-eight lodges, the Iron and Steel Roll Hands of the United States had 473

---

[1] " Principles and Policies of the United States Steel Corporation—Statement by E. H. Gary " (pamphlet), p. 10.

[2] Fitch, *op. cit.*, p. 77.

members in fifteen lodges, and the Sons of Vulcan had 3,331 men in eighty-three lodges. The amalgamation was effected in 1876, the new union being called the " National Amalgamated Association of Iron and Steel Workers." [1] By 1882 there were 197 lodges with 16,000 members in this Association. In that year, however, it engaged in a disastrous strike, a complete failure in every respect, and by 1885 the membership had fallen to 5,702. During this same period the Association suffered from the competition of the organizing efforts of the Knights of Labor. In 1885 and 1886 a new boom struck the Association and by 1889 it had regained the 1882 level of 16,000 members. In that year too it won a decisive victory in the Carnegie, Phipps and Company's Homestead works. With this encouragement it reached its highest membership in 1891, 24,068. [2]

The next year marked the beginning of the decline of the Association, for in 1892 was waged the famous Homestead strike against Carnegie Brothers and Company. It is not my purpose to attempt to add anything to the hundreds of pages that have been written on this episode, [3] but it should be recalled that the strike was fought with bitterness on both sides, that the company hired some 300 Pinkertons to guard the works, that a pitched battle between these guards and the strikers took place on July 6, and that troops had to be called in. Most important for this discussion was the clear-cut position taken on July 8 by Mr. Frick, chairman of the Company at that time, in regard to possible future arrangements with the Amalgamated Association. His state-

[1] Fitch, *op. cit.*, pp. 82-86.

[2] *Ibid.*, p. 86.

[3] Accounts of varying degrees of detail and from various points of view may be found in: Bridge, J. H., *The Inside History of the Carnegie Steel Company*, pp. 184-254; Testimony before the Congressional Investigating Committee, Misc. Doc. No. 335, 52nd Congress, 1st Session; Fitch, *op. cit.*, pp. 122-132.

ment was: " I can say with greatest emphasis that under no circumstances will we have any further dealings with the Amalgamated Association as an organization. This is final." [1] That this " no-conference " attitude has persisted in the Carnegie's lineal descendant, the Corporation, will soon become clear.

All of the different accounts that have been referred to make it clear that the unions had for the most part been exceedingly aggressive down to 1892. A number of students of the question hold that the situation had become intolerable and that the unions had to be smashed. [2]

By 1894 the membership of the Amalgamated had fallen to 10,000, at about which figure it remained until 1900. During these years practically all of the steel mills and most of the iron mills of the Pittsburgh district dislodged the union, so that it retained its place only in the iron mills of the Western Bar Iron Association and in the steel mills of Ohio and Illinois. [3] Just before the formation of the Corporation the Amalgamated showed some signs of returning to its old aggressiveness. The numerous consolidations in the industry in the late nineties doubtless prompted the following constitutional amendment, adopted in 1900: " Should one mill in a combine or trust have a difficulty, all mills in said combine or trust shall cease work until such grievance is settled." [4] On the other side of the controversy we find

---

[1] Pittsburgh *Post*, July 8, 1892. Quoted by Fitch, *op. cit.*, p. 125.

[2] *Cf.* Professor John R. Commons in *Charities and the Commons*, vol. xxi, p. 1064: "For the sake of both the manufacturer and the laborer the union, which had overreached itself and was headstrong in its power, had to be whipped and thrown out." In the next sentence he points out that " Since that time the manufacturers have gone to as mad an extreme in bearing down on their employes as the employes had previously gone in throttling the employer."

[3] *Cf.* on this section Fitch, *op. cit.*, chs. 8, 9 and 10; Neill, *op. cit.*, vol. iii, pp. 111-116.

[4] Constitution of the Amalgamated Association of Iron, Steel and Tin Workers, art. 17, sec. 22. Quoted in Neill, *op. cit.*, vol. iii, p. 116.

recorded in the minutes of the executive committee of the Corporation for June 17, 1901, the following resolution:

That we are unalterably opposed to any extension of union labor and advise subsidiary companies to take firm position when these questions come up and say that they are not going to recognize it, that is, any extension of unions in mills where they do not now exist; that great care should be used to prevent trouble and that they promptly report and confer with this Corporation.[1]

The president of the Corporation was instructed to convey this resolution to the presidents of the various subsidiary corporations.

There are several points to notice in this resolution. First, the subsidiaries are to take a "firm position" and are to "say that they are not going to recognize any extension of unions." In other words within the organization there were no euphemisms: the subsidiaries are definitely ordered to "combat unions as such." Second, it is clear that labor questions of real significance were not to be left to the individual subsidiary but were to be settled by the Corporation. This second point is very important because, as other entries in these same minutes prove, the Corporation was anxious that the public and the unions believe that labor matters were left to the individual subsidiaries. For example, on April 20, 1901, we find this entry:

Mr. Edenborn thinks it expedient to inform the newspapers and the public generally that the United States Steel Corporation is not the one employer, but that the individual companies are distinct and separate for themselves; that the labor troubles of any one company must be settled by that particular company as an individual company, and a strike in one must be settled independently of any other company.[2]

[1] Neill, *op. cit.*, vol. iii, p. 500.

[2] *Ibid.*, p. 497.

On June 17, 1901, in a discussion concerning the advisability of establishing the set rule quoted above for the guidance of subsidiary presidents on the question of recognition of unions in a mill previously not unionized, we find the following:

It has been suggested in this committee that when that question comes up the president of the subsidiary company should reply that he wished to consider and would make answer the next day, and in the meantime could take it up with the president of this company [the Corporation], and then finally report to the representative that the matter had been carefully considered and the decision reached is so and so.

To this last proposition the president commented that it would then be perfectly clear that such president had taken it up with this Corporation.[1]

And from this it is also " perfectly clear " to a reader of the minutes that the Corporation did not want the facts known. Most clear of all, however, are the minutes for July 6, 1901, in which the executive committee is considering the advisability of sending representatives to meet with those of the Amalgamated Association of Iron, Steel and Tin Workers.

The chairman stated that it should be clearly understood that the United States Steel Corporation has nothing whatever to do with it; that the representatives of the three subsidiary companies are not to state that they are acting in concert, or even by consultation, with any of the officials of the United States Steel Corporation.[2]

Thus the ultimate authority on labor questions was vested in the executive committee of the Corporation in 1901. The minutes for this same day, July 6, however, give some indication in the following item of another wheel within those

[1] Neill, *op. cit.*, vol. iii, p. 499.
[2] *Ibid.*, p. 502.

shown. " . . . the president stated that he had been assured by the head of the financial house that he will stand by whatever action the president thinks best." [1] That is, on this union question assistance was assured.

A third point to notice is that the Corporation is here objecting only to the extension of unions; it had not yet begun to refuse to negotiate with them. This " go-easy " policy is, in fact, definitely stated in the minutes for April 20, 1901. After a rather lengthy discussion of the whole matter

. . . it was decided that the sense of this committee is that the general policy should be to temporize for the next six months or a year until we get fully established, and that the prevalent conditions of labor and labor unions at the different plants should be undisturbed, and that if any changes do occur later they can be handled individually.[2]

Of course it must be remembered that there were differences of opinion among the members of the committee, but in general the minutes seem to prove:

1. that the determination of the labor policy was vested in the executive committee;

2. that this committee was opposed to the extension of unions;

3. that despite this opposition it realized the necessity of going slowly.

Here then was the situation in 1901. The Amalgamated had recently adopted a more aggressive attitude because anything short of it seemed a complete surrender of the whole issue. Its officers believed that if these new combinations of employers were to be successfully combatted, the sooner the conflict began the better chances they had. Moreover, it was commonly believed by men closely in touch with the

[1] Neill, *op. cit.*, vol. iii, p. 503.
[2] *Ibid.*, p. 497.

situation at the time that the issue was more or less forced by President Shaffer of the Amalgamated with the idea of enhancing his prestige as a labor leader. On the other hand was the Steel Corporation, opposed to unions, but anxious to avoid trouble during its first critical year, and hence willing to temporize.

The immediate causes which precipitated the strike of 1901 are about as follows. The American Tin Plate Company had for a number of years signed a scale with the Amalgamated for all its plants except one in Monessen. The American Sheet Steel Company, on the other hand, had never signed for more than three-fourths of its mills. Of the twenty union mills it was signed for in 1900-1901 only eleven were at work, and of the nine idle mills four were dismantled in 1901 and 1902 and a fifth in 1904. Of the seven nonunion mills all were at work.[1] In 1900 a rather half-hearted attempt had been made to get the American Sheet Steel Company to sign for all its mills but nothing came of it. In 1901 the Amalgamated was determined to secure all the mills of both these companies. It negotiated first with the American Tin Plate Company, and an agreement on the wage rate was promptly reached. The Company refused to extend the agreement to the Monessen plant on the ground that it was even now signing for a larger percentage of its mills than its competitor the American Sheet Steel Company. [Both were Corporation subsidiaries]. Finally the scale was signed for all mills except Monessen, with the oral agreement, according to the Amalgamated, that it should be included later should the American Sheet Steel Company sign for all 'ts mills. On June 26 negotia-

---

[1] This practice of signing for certain mills and then closing them while the nonunion mills remained in operation was a regular affair and had been utilized as a method of virtually abrogating agreements prior to the formation of the Corporation. *Cf.* Neill, *op. cit.*, vol. iii, p. 119.

tions with that concern began. The Amalgamated demanded the extension of the union to all its mills. The Company replied with a counter-proposition which would make nonunion two mills for which the scale had previously been signed. Neither of these mills had operated the previous year, but the Amalgamated was unable to secure any concessions from the Company and after a second conference on June 29 a strike was ordered on July 1, 1901, against the American Sheet Steel Company and the American Steel Hoop Company. On the same date the American Tin Plate Company was notified that since it was a part of the Corporation, as were these other companies against which the strike was declared, the Amalgamated would be compelled to call out their men should an agreement not be reached by July 8, 1901. This was done in spite of the fact that the scale had been signed with the Tin Plate Company only a few days before.

At this juncture a conference was arranged between representatives of the three companies and the Amalgamated, ostensibly by the individual companies, but actually by the Corporation. This conference in Pittsburgh, July 11, 12, and 13, accomplished nothing in spite of an offer on the part of the American Sheet Steel Company to sign for six more mills than it had the preceding year. The Amalgamated foolishly insisted on all mills of the three companies (particularly calling attention to the fact that a number of men had come out of the hoop mills and stood to gain nothing by the proposed settlement) and since this was refused, carried out the intention of striking the mills of the American Tin Plate Company effective July 15, 1901. The response was not unanimous for various reasons, and the strike was settled in the middle of September by an agreement which cost the Amalgamated fourteen mills of the American Tin Plate Company, a practical withdrawal of the provision of the constitution concerning sympathetic strikes, a promise to refrain from attempts to organize new mills, the practical loss of the right to proselyte among the non-union men in a union mill, and about $1,500,000 in expenses and wages lost.

From the strike of 1901 some three years elapsed before any event of importance to this discussion occurred. In 1904, however, the Carnegie Steel Company, into which had been merged the American Steel Hoop Company, offered the Amalgamated a scale of wages for these hoop mills which was so unsatisfactory that a strike was called. It was lost and, as President McArdle of the Amalgamated expressed it, " that wound up organized labor, . . . in the plants of the Carnegie Steel Company." [1]

There were no more serious breaks until 1909, a period of quiescence secured according to President M. F. Tighe of the Amalgamated, by " giving way to every request that was made by the subsidiary companies when they insisted upon it." [2]   During the whole period from 1902 to 1909, however, the Amalgamated had lost one mill after another so that in 1908 only fourteen of the Steel Corporation's mills were recognized as union mills and of these two had been definitely abandoned.   On June 1, 1909, the American Sheet and Tin Plate Company—a merger of the American Sheet Steel Company and the American Tin Plate Company— served notice in these fourteen mills that after June 30, 1909, they would all be operated as " open " plants. At the same time the company announced a general reduction in wages, averaging 3.5 to 4 per cent and running in some cases as high as 8.8 per cent, and the abolition of the sliding-

---

[1] *Stanley Hearings*, 1911, vol. iv, p. 3136. It will be recalled that unions had been eliminated from the Carnegie mills in the famous Homestead strike of 1892. The acquisition of these new properties had temporarily restored them, but not for long.

[2] *Senate Hearings*, 1919, p. 342.

scale system. The attempts of the Amalgamated to secure a conference with the officials of the subsidiary and later with those of the Corporation were refused. On July 1, 1909, all of the mills except one were struck and many non-union men came out in sympathy. The strike was finally called off on August 27, 1910. It was a complete failure and marked the elimination of unions from the mills of the United States Steel Corporation.[1]

From this time until the movements which developed into the strike of 1919 the question of unions in Corporation mills was dormant. What then gave the impetus to this organization movement?

To this question it seems to me there can be but one answer; though that answer is not the one given by the Corporation, viz., that the whole thing was a Bolshevist plot to overthrow the established institutions of the country, incidentally securing the closed shop in the steel industry and raising certain individuals to positions of power.[2] The vital

---

[1] *Cf.* on this section Neill, *op. cit.*, vol. iii, pp. 120-134; and Fitch, *op. cit.*, pp. 133-136.

[2] That this was the "official" interpretation by the Corporation there can be no doubt. In an interview with members of the Interchurch Commission, Mr. Gary stated that the workmen who "followed the leadership of Fitzpatrick and Foster were Bolsheviki" and that the aims of the strike were "the closed shop, soviets and the forcible distribution of property." (*Report*, p. 33.) In his address to the annual meeting of the stockholders on April 19, 1920, Mr. Gary said: "At present there is more or less social disturbance in this country. There has been a bold, deliberate underhanded movement instituted by people who are not loyal to the principles of our government. Those leading and directing it seek to bring about a revolution, by precipitating industrial strikes and to secure the cooperation of a very great number of men who do not understand the real purpose." (Pamphlet report of Mr. Gary's address, p. 18.) A perusal of the newspapers during the strike could leave the reader with no other impression than that held by the Corporation officials. During the progress of the strike Mr. Fitch reviewed the situation for the *Survey*. He particularly endeavored to find the basis of this "Red" story and interrogated citizens,

point is that during the World War organized labor had made considerable advances, in the packing industry, for example, and in the recognition by the Federal government of the principle of collective bargaining. Workmen were being told that they and their services were as essential to a successful prosecution of the war as the soldiers; they were receiving larger money wages than they ever had before; their complaints and grievances were receiving prompt attention. Thus assured by their employers and their government of their great importance, the workmen began to be-

mill officials, and public officials but in no case got any *evidence* of the claim that the strike was a revolution. When pinned down they uniformly referred to "the newspapers." (*Survey*, November 8, 1919.) The Interchurch Commission also endeavored to find the facts concerning this "plot," particularly from steel executives, but reported that it got no evidence. (*Cf.* the *Report*, pp. 32, 33 *et seq.*) Major-General Leonard Wood, in charge of the situation at Gary, Indiana, after martial law was declared, was quoted as saying that the Reds who were making the trouble at Gary were not fomenting the strike and had no interest in the industrial struggle as such, but went there because of the opportunities for misleading a lot of men who were engaged in an economic controversy and inflaming them into acts of violence. (*New York Times,* October 19, 1919.) As a matter of fact most of the hue and cry was founded directly or indirectly upon the fact that Mr. Foster was and is a radical and that he introduced in the Chicago Federation of Labor the resolution that started the organizing campaign. The present writer's study of the facts convinces him that the Corporation's interpretation of the nature of the strike was incorrect, that it was simply a convenient tool ready to hand because of the post-war hysteria against radicals of all sorts. In commenting on this situation and on the attitude of business men and newspapers when faced by the industrial disturbances that followed the armistice, Mr. Frank Cobb said, "Instead of trying to get at the basic cause of it all, they adopted the primitive medicine man procedure of hunting out the devil upon whom the responsibility could be laid. Four hundred thousand steel workers had gone out because the leader of the strike had once been a syndicalist. All the shipping in New York was tied up because I. W. W. agitators had taken possession of 80,000 longshoremen. . . . Nothing in this complicated world is ever quite so simple as that." (Address before the Women's City Club of New York on December 11, 1919. Printed as Senate Document 175 of the 66th Congress, second session. *Cf.* p. 11.)

lieve it themselves. The organizer found them ready to accept the union which they hoped would solidify and maintain their war gains. That these facts were appreciated is shown in the following statement by William Z. Foster:

> But as the war wore on . . . the situation changed rapidly in favor of the unions. The demand for soldiers and munitions had made labor scarce; the Federal administration was friendly; . . . the steel industry was the master-clock of the whole war program and had to be kept in operation at all costs. . . . It was an opportunity to organize the industry such as might never again occur.[1]

In the light of the situation Mr. Foster presented to the Chicago Federation of Labor on April 7, 1918, a resolution calling upon the executive officers of the American Federation of Labor to inaugurate a national campaign to organize the steel workers.[2] This resolution was introduced by the Chicago Federation at the June, 1918, convention of the American Federation of Labor and unanimously carried. Pursuant to the instructions of the convention, Mr. Gompers, president of the American Federation of Labor, called a meeting for August 1, in Chicago, of representatives of all the unions interested in organizing steel. Twenty-four unions answered the call; a National Committee for Organizing Iron and Steel Workers, composed of one representative of each of the unions with Mr. Gompers as chairman and Mr. Foster as secretary-treasurer, was organized; a uniform initiation fee (except for bricklayers, molders, and pattern-makers) was agreed upon; and each union appropriated $100 for conducting the organizing campaign.[3]

[1] Foster, Wm. Z., *The Great Steel Strike and Its Lessons* (New York, 1920), p. 17. On the preceding page the third sub-head for the chapter is "A Golden Chance."

[2] *Ibid.*, p. 17.

[3] *Senate Hearings*, 1919, p. 8; Foster, *op. cit.*, pp. 16-24, *passim*.

The inadequacy of this sum for the task of getting half a million men into unions forced a complete change of the organizing plans. The original intention was to start the campaign simultaneously in all important steel centers, making more or less of a "whirlwind" drive of it; but neither the men nor the money were available, and consequently activities were at first restricted to the so-called Calumet district including South Chicago, Gary, Joliet, Indiana Harbor, and a few lesser points. Actual work began in September and, according to the union leaders, the above-named centers responded so promptly that an organization was soon established.[1] Doubtless some allowance should be made for the optimism of Mr. Fitzpatrick and Mr. Foster in these statements, but the fact remains that enough progress was made to cause the steel executives considerable worry. On October 1, 1918, the Corporation, followed by many of the independents, inaugurated the basic eight-hour day.[2] One of the chief arguments of organizers was that they hoped to eliminate the twelve-hour day from the industry and establish a universal eight-hour day. On the face of it the action taken by the employers seems a deliberate attempt to meet this, though it must be remembered that the "basic" eight-hour day really had nothing at all to do with hours but was simply a method of wage payment that gave "time and a half" for all work over eight hours. This system was, of course, particularly advantageous to the men on twelve hours, since it was equivalent to a sixteen and two-thirds per cent increase in pay.

By this time the National Committee was receiving requests from men in the Pittsburgh districts for organizers.

[1] *Senate Hearings*, 1919, p. 8; Foster, *op. cit.*, p. 26. Foster states that "In Gary 749 joined at the first meeting, Joliet enrolled 500, and other places did almost as well."

[2] Foster claimed that the Corporation had only a short time before issued definite statements that no such step would be taken. *Cf. The Great Steel Strike*, p. 27.

Encouraged by developments to date the organizing movement was expanded so that despite the handicaps of the influenza epidemic and opposition from local authorities in some towns [1] the new members added to the unions involved were " something like 80,000 " in May, 1919. In this month the National Convention of the Amalgamated Association of Iron, Steel and Tin Workers, the union most vitally interested, of course, met in Louisville, Kentucky. The convention instructed Mr. M. F. Tighe, president of the Amalgamated, to write to Mr. Gary in the endeavor to arrange a conference. The conference was refused on the usual ground that the Corporation did not confer with labor unions as such.[2]

From here on events moved more rapidly. The 1919 convention of the A. F. of L., held in Atlantic City in June, received a report stating that upwards of 100,000 men had joined one or the other of the unions involved. Thereupon it authorized Mr. Gompers to endeavor to arrange a conference between Mr. Gary and an executive committee from the National Committee.[3] Immediately after the close of the convention Mr. Gompers wrote to Mr. Gary stating the progress made in organizing the steel workers and requesting Mr. Gary to meet the executive committee.[4] This com-

---

[1] This and similar points will be discussed in detail in the next chapter: "Methods by which the Corporation secured and maintained a non-union organization"; see pp. 111 *et seq.*

[2] The correspondence will be found in the *Senate Hearings*, 1919, p. 368 and in Foster, *op. cit.*, pp. 70-72. Mr. Tighe insisted on putting these letters into the record because he believed his letter " shows conclusively what efforts were made in order to effect a conciliation." Mr. Foster characterizes the move as " a bid for separate consideration by the steel companies " (p. 69), and an " attempt at desertion." (p. 72.)

[3] Mr. Gompers resigned as chairman of this committee at the Atlantic City meeting. His place was taken by John Fitzpatrick, president of the Chicago Federation of Labor. *Senate Hearings*, 1919, p. 94.

[4] Mr. Gompers's letter of June 20 is printed in *Senate Hearings*, 1919, p. 224; Foster, *op. cit.*, pp. 74, 75.

munication Mr. Gary did not trouble himself to answer. Organization work went forward. On July 24 at a meeting of representatives of the unions interested it was agreed that since it seemed impossible to secure a conference with Mr. Gary as matters stood, the next step was to take a strike vote of the men which should authorize the National Committee for Organizing Iron and Steel Workers to take what action it saw fit in the event that the " no-conference " attitude was maintained. The next meeting was scheduled for August 20, by which time the strike vote was to be completed. The returns from it showed that 98 per cent of the men who voted favored a strike.[1] Reinforced by this vote the executive committee went to Mr. Gary's office in New York on August 26. They were requested to present their business in writing since Mr. Gary " wished to be excused from a personal interview." The committee's letter was nothing more than a request for a conference on matters at issue, but Mr. Gary refused to see them in a letter of August 27, chiefly because he contended that they did not represent the sentiment of a majority of the Corporation's employees, and, secondly, because the Corporation never dealt with unions as such. In their reply the committee stated that they could prove they represented the men only by calling them out on strike, a thing they hoped to avoid, that Mr. Gary's " no-conference " attitude seemed unreasonable to them, and that they believed him to be misinformed on certain important topics.[2]

Blocked in New York the group returned to Washington,

[1] *Senate Hearings*, 1919, p. 13. It should be noted that each union tabulated its votes independently so that all the National Committee received was a statement that a certain percentage of men favored the strike in each union. The actual figures were never made public. See pp. 14 and 383, testimony of Mr. Fitzpatrick and Mr. Foster.

[2] The letters were printed in *Senate Hearings*, 1919, pp. 16-18, and in Foster, *op. cit.*, pp. 79-83.

spent August 28 in conference with Mr. Gompers and other
A. F. of L. officials, and on the following day saw President
Wilson. Although the President agreed to attempt to arrange a conference with Mr. Gary for the executive committee, he was unable to do so, and the union leaders on
September 10 set the strike for September 22.[1] The President's next move was to telegraph Mr. Gompers on the day
the strike date was set, requesting a postponement of the
strike until after the Industrial Conference scheduled for
October 6. This telegram Mr. Gompers forwarded to Mr.
Fitzpatrick at the same time expressing the " hope that
something can be done without injury to the workers and
their cause to endeavor to conform to the wish expressed by
the President." [2] Copies of Mr. Gompers's letter also went
to the presidents of the unions involved. At first some of
these were inclined to accede to President Wilson's request,
but after a conference in Pittsburgh they unanimously re-
affirmed September 22 as the strike date. The two chief
reasons for this decision were: first, that the leaders were
convinced that a postponement would mean a more or less
complete disintegration of the organization and the loss of
the confidence of the workmen; and, second, that a considerable body of the men would strike regardless of any action
taken by the National Committee for Organizing Iron and
Steel Workers.[3] Since no concessions and no definite hopes
for them were apparent they believed there was much more

[1] On the interchange of telegrams between the President and the committee compare Mr. Fitzpatrick's testimony, *Senate Hearings,* 1919, p. 30;
Mr. Gompers's, *ibid.,* p. 107; and Foster, *op. cit.,* pp. 84-87.

[2] *Senate Hearings,* 1919, p. 4.

[3] *Senate Hearings,* 1919, pp. 108, 109. Foster, *op. cit.,* pp. 90-93. Foster
states that the local unions "notified the National Committee that they
were going to strike on September 22, regardless of anything that body
might do short of getting them definite concessions and protection."
(p. 91.) All the strike leaders agreed in emphasizing the "wholesale
discharge" of union men as an important factor.

to be lost than gained by postponement. This conclusion and the evidence supporting it the executive group of the National Committee set forth in a letter of September 18 to President Wilson.[1]

Officially, the strike lasted from September 22, 1919, to January 8, 1920; actually, the heart was taken out of it long before that. The National Committee claimed to have 365,-600 men on strike on September 29, and 109,300 on December 10.[2] It is probable that both of these figures are too high, but the significant fact is that the second is less than one-third the first. The men returned to work without gaining any of their demands; in practically every respect the strike had been a failure. The reasons for its failure are to some extent a matter of controversy, but in general it may be said that the immense size, wealth, and power of the industry, and particularly of the Corporation, rendered its position impregnable against an attack that was weakened by a lack of funds and by a lack of unity from the beginning. Foster himself states bluntly that the responsibility for the failure of the strike rests " upon the shoulders of Organized Labor." [3] His chief points are the impossibility of organizing steel on a craft basis and the lack of team-work between the unions that entered the campaign. But the relative merits of craft and industrial unionism and the internal dissensions in the group directing the strike of 1919 are not matters of primary interest here. More important is the explanation of the position the Corporation had secured, a topic with which the next chapter is concerned.

[1] *Senate Hearings*, 1919, pp. 5, 6, 7.

[2] Foster, *op. cit.*, p. 191.

[3] *Ibid.*, p. 234.

CHAPTER IV

Methods by which the Corporation Secured and Maintained a Nonunion Organization

In the preceding chapter have been sketched chronologically the developments by which the unions were first eliminated and subsequently largely barred from Corporation mills. The methods by which these results were accomplished are discussed below. Some of them are admitted by Corporation officials, some have been established by independent investigations, and others are of such a nature that they may be considered inherent in the situation and so are not particularly " Corporation " methods, or have been the ground of so much controversy that they should perhaps be classified as " alleged " methods. The first two groups include :

1. Closing mills after signing a scale for them.
2. Using convict labor.
3. Engaging spies to report on " labor agitators ".
4. Engaging strike-breakers.
5. Discharging men for union activities.
6. Blacklisting men for union activities.

Among the latter methods are :

1. Employment of foreign in preference to native labor.
2. Control of the press.
3. Control of public officials.
4. Inauguration of " welfare " programs.

The first method of fighting unions, closing mills after signing the scale for them, was mentioned in the preceding chapter,[1] where it was pointed out that of the twenty mills for which the American Sheet Steel Company was signed in 1900-1901 only eleven were at work, and that of the seven nonunion mills all were at work. Moreover, there were 68 stands of rolls in the seven nonunion mills and only 67 in the eleven union mills that were in operation.[2] Additional evidence on this point is contained in the minutes of the executive committee for July 2, 1901, during a discussion of the advisability of conceding to the Amalgamated three mills previously nonunion, in which the chairman stated " that he would be willing to concede two mills as union mills, to sign the scale for the McKeesport mill and to keep it shut down ".[3] This method has, of course, not been used since 1909 when unions were eliminated.

A second method of checking unions, the use of convict labor in mining properties of the Corporation, is now obsolete, was never extensive, and is inserted here primarily in an endeavor to make the record complete.

During the progress of the Stanley investigation in 1911 Mr. Shelby M. Harrison, writer for the *Survey*, testified that the " advantages " of convict labor as explained to him " by a number of employers " were as follows:

(1) that it was cheaper or at least as cheap as free labor,
(2) that it was more regular,
(3) that it was " a block toward the growth of labor unions in the district ".

Speaking specifically of Mr. George G. Crawford, president of a Corporation subsidiary, Mr. Harrison said:

[1] P. 100.
[2] Neill, *op. cit.,* vol. iii, p. 121.
[3] *Ibid.,* p. 502.

The president of the Tennessee Co. told me frankly that he
thought that the employing of convict labor in the district was
a block toward unionism. He was fair-minded enough, however, to say that he thought they ought not to have that leverage
over the unions.[1]

Since Mr. Harrison was in the Birmingham district in May
and June of 1911 [2] the statements attributed to Mr. Crawford were most probably made at that time. Some months
later the contract with the state of Alabama for the use of
convicts in the Tennessee Company's mines expired and
through a misunderstanding, the details of which are immaterial, the Tennessee Company was not allotted any state
convicts after January 1, 1912. Mr. Crawford protested
vigorously to Mr. J. G. Oakley, chairman of the Board of
Convict Inspectors, in a letter of November 24, 1911, partly
on the ground that his company would be put to considerable expense in building houses for free labor and in collect-
ing a labor force on relatively short notice. In explaining
why he had retained the convict system when he became
president Mr. Crawford stated that " the chief inducement
for the hiring of convicts was the certainty of a supply of
coal for our manufacturing operations in the contingency of
labor troubles. . . ." [3] Mr. Oakley testified that a " very
strenuous effort " was made to convince the governor, who
had the power to cancel these convict contracts, that the
contract which had supplanted that with the Tennessee Com-

---

[1] *Stanley Hearings,* 1911, vol. iv, p. 2982.

[2] *Cf. ibid.,* p. 2962.

[3] *Stanley Hearings,* 1911, vol iv, p. 3112. It may be contended that
this use of convict labor was a hang-over from a time prior to the
purchase of the Tennessee Company by the Corporation, and that, consequently, the latter can not be held responsible; but this appears to
me to be a quibble. All major questions of labor policy were settled
by the executive committee of the Corporation. *Cf.* pp. 97-99, *supra.*

pany was not as advantageous to the state as the Tennessee's contract.[1]

The use of labor spies in the anti-union crusade of employers who are advocates of the " open " shop is a matter of common knowledge among all students of the labor problem. Generally speaking, labor spies are of two classes: those maintained in the employ of a corporation as a part of the ordinary force, and those hired from some agency for an emergency of short or long duration. That the United States Steel Corporation has utilized both sorts throughout its history is easily demonstrated.

As pointed out in the introductory chapter of this study, one of the reasons for the formation of the Corporation was a desire to integrate the operations in that part of the industry controlled by the combination. A part of this policy included the ownership and operation of the Pittsburgh Steamship Company, a concern operating on the Great Lakes. Mr. Harry Coulby, president of the Company, has "dominated the labor policy of the Lake Carriers' Association since December, 1903." [2] As a part of this labor policy, dominated by the head of a Corporation subsidiary,

. . . the individual owners and the association, through various kinds of spy systems, keep in close touch with the activities of unions and of the men most prominent in them. Hence it is possible at any time to remove men who make trouble, whether in the cause of unionism or otherwise.[3]

The evidence relating to the steel works is, of course, more detailed. During the progress of the Pittsburgh Survey Mr. Fitch became convinced that " all of the steel com-

---

[1] *Stanley Hearings*, 1911, vol. iv, p. 3113.

[2] Hoagland, H. E., *Wage Bargaining on the Vessels of the Great Lakes* (Urbana, Illinois, 1917), p. 60.

[3] *Ibid.*, p. 95.

panies have effective methods of learning what is going on among the workmen," and that "... the United States Steel Corporation has regular secret service departments."[1] Time after time he found that if the "conversation be shifted to the steel works" the men "immediately become reticent". From these experiences the conclusions reached may best be put in the words of Mr. Fitch:

I doubt whether you could find a more suspicious body of men than the employes of the United States Steel Corporation. They are suspicious of one another, of their neighbors, and of their friends. I was repeatedly suspected of being an agent of the Corporation, sent out to sound the men with regard to their attitude toward the Corporation and toward unionism.[2]

During the time that unions persisted in some plants of the Corporation it was evidently the practice to maintain a spy or spies within the organization. On this point the following extract from Mr. Fitch's testimony to the Stanley Committee is convincing:

Lewellyn Lewis was, two years ago, a vice president of the Amalgamated Association of Iron and Steel Workers. He told me last fall that some time ago—he did not say just when—a meeting of delegates of various locals of the union was held in Youngstown, Ohio, to consider a wage scale. Mr. Lewis for some reason was unable to attend the meeting. He arranged with one of the men to call him over the long-distance telephone at his home in Martins Ferry, Ohio, and tell him just what action was taken. He said across the river in Wheeling, W. Va., a district manager of the American Sheet and Tin Plate Co. lived, and that in the afternoon of the day this meeting was held in Youngstown this district manager called Mr. Lewis up on the telephone and said that he would tell him what action

[1] Fitch, *op. cit.*, p. 219.
[2] *Ibid.*, p. 214.

had been taken in Youngstown. He did give him the scale of wages that had been agreed upon and also told him how all the locals had voted. Mr. Lewis said a few minutes after that his own man in Youngstown called him on the long-distance telephone and gave him exactly the same information, and that the official of the steel company across the river had been right in every detail.[1]

Subsequent to the date of Mr. Fitch's work are the report of the Federal Industrial Relations Commission (1915) including the special report of Mr. Luke Grant on the use of spies by the National Erectors' Association of which Corporation subsidiaries were members, and the series of articles by Mr. Sidney Howard on " The Labor Spy " published in the *New Republic* in the early months of 1921. These indicate not only the retention but the expansion of the use of labor spies in industry in general, and the steel industry in particular. During the Interchurch investigation one of their representatives was furnished the " labor file " of a steel company in Monessen, Pennsylvania, that established beyond question the fact that Corporation plants regularly exchanged " under-cover " information secured by the hired " operatives " of so-called detective agencies with other plants in the district.[2] If any further proof is needed it is found in the following extract from the record of the 1919 investigation.

Senator Walsh. Have you a secret-service organization among your employees at any of the subsidiary plants of the Steel Corporation?

Mr. Gary. Well, Senator, I cannot be very specific about that, but I am quite sure that at times some of our people have used secret-service men to ascertain facts and conditions.[3]

[1] *Stanley Hearings*, 1911, vol. iv, p. 2885.
[2] *Cf. Public Opinion and the Steel Strike*, p. 7 et seq.
[3] *Senate Hearings*, 1919, p. 177.

The question arises, then, if the use of spies is admitted, why spend so much time upon the matter? A more detailed answer is reserved for the conclusions of this study, but at this point it may be noted that the facts indicate that some of the methods actually used by the Corporation are in unpleasant contrast with statements made by Judge Gary and other officials in reference to its labor policy. Typical of such statements is the following:

But I make the assertion, gentlemen, that in no line of industry, at any period in the history of the world in any country, was labor on the whole better treated in every respect than it is at the present time by the employers of labor in this great line of industrial activity.[1]

Closely connected with the system of industrial espionage is the use of strike-breakers. As a matter of fact one of the most important services performed by the spy is strike-breaking, not so much by actually doing the work the union man has left as by creating dissension among strikers and spreading a defeatist sentiment that will send the men back to work. Typical of the former method of attack is the letter sent out by the Sherman Service to one of their operatives on October 2, 1919.

We want you to stir up as much bad feeling as you possibly can between the Serbians and Italians. Spread data among the Serbians that the Italians are going back to work. Call up every question you can in reference to racial hatred between these two nationalities: make them realize to the fullest extent that far better results would be accomplished if they will go back to work. Urge them to go back to work or the Italians will get their jobs.[2]

[1] From Mr. Gary's address to the Iron and Steel Institute on May 17, 1912. Printed in *Senate Hearings, 1919*, p. 237.

[2] *Public Opinion and the Steel Strike*, pp. 58-59.

The Interchurch Commission of Inquiry was informed by the president of the Illinois Steel Company, a Corporation subsidiary, that his company had not engaged the Sherman Service; but was told by the business director of the Service that Sherman operatives were hired by the Illinois Steel Company.[1] The activities of the Sherman Service finally became so obnoxious that on complaint of the Chicago Federation of Labor their offices were raided and sufficient evidence secured to indict " advisory director " H. V. Phillips on charges of conspiracy to " riot ", " insurrection ", and " murder ".[2] The indictment was subsequently quashed, but nevertheless the evidence seems to indicate that the methods of these agencies have not materially improved in the period since the United States Commission on Industrial Relations recommended that because of their " endless crimes " they be compelled to operate under a Federal license under strict supervision or be " utterly abolished ".[3]

The other phase of strike-breaking, the employment of new men, often imported from other localities, has also been a more or less common practice of the United States Steel Corporation, as, indeed, it is with many employers. As far back as 1892 the importation of strike-breakers and Pinkertons by the Carnegie people was the immediate cause of the disgraceful Homestead riot. Mr. P. J. McArdle, at one time president of the Amalgamated Association of Iron, Steel and Tin Workers, testified in 1911 that during the strike of 1909 the American Sheet and Tin Plate Company offered special inducements to secure strike-breakers.[4] So far as I

---

[1] *Public Opinion and the Steel Strike*, pp. 61 and 62. Whether this particular concern was engaged by the Corporation is not material, of course, for similar agencies were engaged whose practices were much the same. *Cf.* pp. 7 and 8.

[2] *Ibid.*, pp. 57 and 60.

[3] Final Report, vol. i, p. 57.

[4] *Stanley Hearings*, 1911, vol. iv, p. 3120.

have been able to ascertain, this charge was never denied by
Corporation officials. During the 1919 strike the weight of
the available evidence indicates that strike-breakers were
used quite generally by Corporation and independent mills
alike. Mr. Foster states that " National Committee secretaries' reports indicate that the Steel Trust recruited and
shipped from 30,000 to 40,000 negroes into the mills as
strike-breakers." [1] The Interchurch *Report on the Steel
Strike of 1919* listed among the reasons for the failure of
the strike ". . . the successful use of strike-breakers, principally negroes, . . . Negro workers were imported and were
shifted from plant to plant: in Gary the negroes were
marched ostentatiously through the streets; in Youngstown
and near Pittsburgh they were smuggled in at night ".
This information was secured, in part at least, from employers: " ' Niggers did it,' was a not uncommon remark
among company officers ".[2]

Mr. O. E. Anderson, president of Hustler Lodge number
thirty-six of the Amalgamated Association of Iron, Steel
and Tin Workers in Gary, Indiana, testified that a large
number of men, mostly negroes, had been brought into Gary
as strike-breakers.[3] On the other hand, Mr. L. W. Mc-
Namee, auditor of the Gary works of the Illinois Steel Company, stated that " The companies made no efforts to bring
in strike-breakers at all." [4] Both these statements were
made under oath and both men probably believed they were
stating the truth, but the evidence previously cited plus the
statements of reporters and investigators in newspapers and

[1] Foster, *op. cit.*, p. 207. By " Steel Trust" Mr. Foster refers to the
" collectivity of the great steel Companies," not the Corporation alone.

[2] Pp. 177 and 178.

[3] *Senate Hearings*, 1919, p. 956.

[4] *Ibid.*, p. 1045. Mr. McNamee was referring only to the Gary plants
in this statement.

magazines during and immediately after the strike is convincing proof that the Corporation used strike-breakers freely.[1]

A fifth, and, according to the men, a very common instrument for fighting unions is the power of discharge. Mr. Gary testified to the Senate Committee in 1919 as follows:

We have known that we had a good many union men, of course. While it has been said we discharged them and tried to get rid of them, there is no foundation for that statement. If that has ever been done in a single case or in a few cases, if it has ever been done, which I deny, it has been contrary to our positive instructions and would not have been permitted, and the man would be disciplined if he disobeyed those instructions the second time.[2]

This is a very positive statement. The Judge says, "There is no foundation for the statement " . . . "if it has *ever* been done, *which I deny,* it has been contrary to our instructions ". It has been impossible to ascertain the date on which these " instructions " were issued, but the resolution passed unanimously by the executive committee, of which Mr. Gary was chairman, stating that the Corporation was " unalterably opposed to any extension of union labor " and advising the " subsidiary companies to take firm position " has been cited.[3] That was June 17, 1901. The superintendents of local mills interpreted " unalterably opposed " and " firm position " as covering discharge for union activities, and on July 8, 1901, the president of the Corporation reported to the executive committee that the

[1] *Survey,* November 8, 1919, *passim. New York Times,* September 23, 24, 26; October 5, 10.

[2] *Senate Hearings,* 1919, p. 166.

[3] P. 97, *supra.*

superintendent of the Wellsville sheet mill had discharged twelve men who were endeavoring to institute a lodge and that Shaffer, the president of the Amalgamated at that time, demanded that they be taken back. After some discussion the committee agreed that this be done, but only because of the exceedingly great desire to prevent trouble at this time. The minutes make it clear that only one man on the committee considered the discharge essentially unjust; the others were deterred from upholding the superintendent only because of the existing circumstances.[1]

Additional light on these " positive instructions " is found in Hoagland's monograph on *Wage-Bargaining on Vessels of the Great Lakes* previously cited. Shortly after the formation of the Corporation it completed arrangements by which it secured control of approximately one-third of the freight-carrying vessels on the Great Lakes through its subsidiary, the Pittsburgh Steamship Company. The president and manager of this company, Mr. Harry Coulby, in an address to the Ship Masters' Association in 1908, said:

What we are trying to do is simply to get back to the old conditions aboard ship. We don't want any members of the crew to see if it is in the Red Book before they do it. You masters have got to go on the picket line; you've got to win this fight for us. For my own company I can say that we are going to win if it takes one day, one month, one year or five years. If any man pulls a book of rules on you he is not an open shop man. Put him on the dock. If any engineer, first, second, or third, wheelsman, watchman, mate declines to obey orders, put him on the dock. We will help you fill their places.[2]

Here is a different sort of " instructions "; those from the president of an important Corporation subsidiary to the

---

[1] Neill, *op. cit.*, vol. iii, p. 503 *et seq.*

[2] Hoagland, *op. cit.*, p. 87; quoted from the *Marine Review* of April 16, 1908.

masters of lake vessels to put all union men on the docks. There is nothing on record to show that Mr. Coulby was ever "disciplined", but it is on record that members of the Lake Carriers' Association have discharged union men " as such " since 1908. The Corporation in this respect has dominated the policy of the Lake Carriers' Association.

Cases of discharge from steel mills for joining a union or for " union activities " such as " proselyting " or " agitating " can be traced straight through the Corporation's history from the case previously cited of the discharge of twelve men from the Wellsville mill in 1901 to the organizing period in 1919. D. P. Boyer, shearman for ten years in the Apollo and Vandergrift mills of the American Sheet and Tin Plate Company, made affidavit that he and his brother-in-law were discharged on September 16, 1909, because their wives had been seen at a union meeting.[1]

The following extract from the testimony to the Stanley Committee cites other cases:

Mr. Young. Do you mean the Steel Corporation has discharged men simply because they joined a labor organization?
Mr. Fitch. Yes.
Mr. Young. Where did that occur?
Mr. Fitch. That occurred at Homestead at a number of different times. It occurred at Gary about a year and a half ago.
The Chairman. Give us that Gary incident, or one of them.
Mr. Fitch. One with which I am particularly familiar is that of a young man working in the electrical department— a young high school boy from a town in Ohio. I talked with him. He was rather a clean-looking young American boy. He had been carrying a book in which the men had been writing their names down because they wanted to join an electrical workers' union. He was acting as secretary pending a formal organization, and was accepting their dues and their member-

---

[1] *Stanley Hearings,* 1911, vol. iv, p. 3151.

ship fees. He had been doing that for about two weeks when he was suddenly discharged, and given a slip upon which he was told to go to the office for his pay. Upon his slip were written the words, " Union agitator." I have seen that slip.[1]

P. H. Brogan testified to the Senate Committee in 1919 that he was discharged on June 30, 1919, from the Clairton works of the Corporation for joining a union.[2]

Joe Kerspinach, a naturalized Austrian, testified during the strike investigation of 1919 that he was discharged from the National Tube Company's (a Corporation subsidiary) works at McKeesport for joining the union.

Senator Walsh. How do you know that you were discharged by reason of being a member of the union?
Mr. Kerspinach. They told me if you get a letter you don't belong to the union you get the job back.
Senator Walsh. Who told you that?
Mr. Kerspinach. The foreman.
Senator Walsh. Who is he?
Mr. Kerspinach. John D. Skelly.[3]

O. E. Anderson, guide-setter in the rail mill of the Illinois Steel Company at Gary, Indiana, testified that a close friend of his, E. A. Luchs, was selected as a delegate to the convention of the Amalgamated Association in May, 1919. Two weeks before the convention he applied to his foreman for a leave of two weeks' duration in which to attend the convention. The leave was granted. On the day before Luchs was to leave, however, the foreman notified him that if he went to the convention he need not come back. Luchs went despite this threat and has been refused employment since.[4]

---

[1] *Stanley Hearings,* 1911, vol. iv, p. 2952.
[2] *Senate Hearings,* 1919, p. 552.
[3] *Ibid.,* p. 726.
[4] *Ibid.,* p. 974.

The Interchurch *Report on the Steel Strike of 1919* states that "Discharges for joining the union were so common in the months before the strike that the union organizers did not even keep records of the cases. Cases were too common to need proving. . . ." An investigator for the Commission in November, 1919, in two days' time secured about 200 signed statements and sworn affidavits from discharged workers who had been told or had good reason to believe that the cause was union affiliation.[1]   Among others from independent companies, the Interchurch *Report* contains the statements of two Corporation employees, John Dablonski of 320½ Syria Street, Duquesne, Pennsylvania, and Joe Mayor, 440 Beach Way, Homestead, Pennsylvania. The latter was asked by his superintendent whether he was at a meeting of the union. Mayor replied:

I was. How do you know?

Supt. Somebody turned your name in and I am going to discharge you.

Mayor. What's matter? What I do, rob company of couple of dollars?

Supt. We don't want you to attend union meetings. I don't want union men to work for me.

When the Superintendent inquired what they had told him at the meeting, he refused to answer and further refused to answer when the Superintendent asked him for the names of others present at the meeting.[2]

Mr. Gary's subordinates were quoted by the Interchurch Commission as follows: " Mr. Buffington of the Illinois Steel, also Mr. Williams' representative for the Carnegie Steel and other officers put it uniformly in these words: ' We don't discharge a man for belonging to a union, but of course we discharge men for agitating in the mills ' ".[3]

[1] Pp. 212 and 213.

[2] Interchurch, *Report on the Steel Strike of 1919,* p. 218.

[3] *Ibid.,* p. 210.

During the early weeks of the 1919 strike the *Survey* sent Mr. Fitch to the steel districts to secure some first hand information. Mr. L. Burnett, assistant to the president of the Carnegie Steel Company, in an interview with Mr. Fitch, " stated that it was the policy of the company to discharge union men who were active or were organizing within the plant ". He further stated that a group had been discharged in Homestead some time before the strike for circulating inside the plant a petition to John Fitzpatrick requesting him to organize them.[1]

But there is no use in further burdening the record. Mr. Gary's positive statement quoted at the beginning of this section seems to be quite at variance with the facts revealed through both public and private investigation into what actually goes on in the mills of the Corporation.

A sixth tool which the Corporation has utilized to smash union activities in its plants is the blacklist. Evidence on this point is scant in quantity but conclusive in character. The Dewees Wood plant of the American Sheet and Tin Plate Company had been the scene of union controversies before it became a part of the Corporation. During the 1901 trouble an unsuccessful effort was made to unionize it. Almost ten years later Mr. Fitch wrote : " When the strike was over the president of the lodge in Wood's Mill was refused re-employment, and today it is a matter of common report that he is blacklisted in every mill of the Steel Corporation." [2]

In 1908 the Pittsburgh Steamship Company inaugurated a " Welfare Plan ", the features of which it is unnecessary to explain in detail. Mr. Hoagland, in the monograph cited before, states that one part of the system, the continuous discharge book, " constituted a very effectual blacklist ".[3] V. A.

---

[1] *Survey*, November 8, 1919, pp. 55, 86.
[2] Fitch, *op. cit.*, p. 218.
[3] Hoagland, *op. cit.*, pp. 88-89.

Olander, secretary of the Lake Seamen's Union, testified to the Stanley Committee that the ratings given by the officers in these discharge books were purely arbitrary and that no union man had a chance to get a satisfactory rating, without which he could not reship.[1] This system was abolished by order of the United States Shipping Board in 1917, but was reintroduced in the spring of 1922.[2] One rather contemptible trick utilized was to hand to employees and prospective employees two slips, one stating that the signer was a union man, the other that he was nonunion. The men were told that since some masters and engineers preferred union men and some preferred nonunion men the Lake Carriers' Association, dominated by the Pittsburgh Steamship Company, was using this method of securing for both groups the workmen they preferred. Speaking of the men who signed the union slips Mr. Olander testified:

Invariably they landed on the dock a very short time afterwards.

A man who signed the union slip in the shipping office had no earthly show to ship. Nothing was said to him. He simply did not ship; that is all.

This was just a trick to get the men to declare themselves. . . . [3]

During the Senate investigation of the 1919 strike an attorney for the strikers submitted the following original letter from the office of the vice-president and general superintendent of the American Steel and Wire Company addressed to Henry Barren, Newburg Steel Works, Cleveland, Ohio:

[1] *Stanley Hearings*, 1911, vol. iv, pp. 3009-3024, *passim*.

[2] Albrecht, A. E., *International Seamen's Union of America* (Washington, 1923), pp. 63, 66.

[3] *Stanley Hearings*, 1911, vol. iv, p. 3014.

Dear Sir: Four rod rollers were discharged from Donora the other day for cause. I understand that one of them, named John Brown, has secured work at Newburg. If you find that this is the case please let him out at once. . . . [1]

This letter was dated March 2, 1909.

The investigators of the Interchurch Commission found a regular blacklisting system in which Corporation and independent plants were joined. The most interesting bit of evidence is, of course, the now famous scrap of dirty paper listing the names of " some Belgian dogs " who made it so hard for the writer that he was compelled to quit his job. Copies of this anonymous missive, discovered in the " labor file " proffered by a steel company in Monessen as explained above, were sent to every steel concern in Monessen, including the American Sheet and Tin [Plate] Company and the Carnegie Steel Company.[2]

In addition to the six methods discussed above that are admitted or for which there is convincing evidence are four others for which the evidence is not so convincing or which may be considered as being a part of the situation. The latter factor seems to be particularly true of the use of foreign workmen with lower standards of living who were willing to accept wages, hours, and conditions that were repugnant to at least a large part of the members of the Amalgamated Association of Iron, Steel, and Tin Workers. It is easy, of course, to establish the fact that during the period the Corporation was driving out the unions the percentage of foreign born workmen in the mills had greatly increased,[3] but it is difficult to establish any desire on the part of Cor-

---

[1] *Senate Hearings*, 1919, p. 735.

[2] *Cf.* the *Report on the Steel Strike of 1919*, pp. 222-225.

[3] The percentage of foreign born in the iron and steel industry in 1900 was 35.9; in 1908 it was 57.7. Neill, *op. cit.*, vol. iii, p. 91. I have found no separate figures for the Corporation.

poration officials in general that this change should take place, and infinitely more difficult to prove that to the extent such a desire existed the purpose behind it was union-smashing. At least two investigators convinced themselves that the Corporation had sought to supplant American with foreign workmen. In speaking of the Lake Carriers' Association's efforts to secure greater stability in its working force Mr. Hoagland says:

> Finally, the Lake Carriers' Association has made conscious and persistent efforts to secure for service on the boats different types of men than formerly worked there. As firemen, the former irresponsible floaters have been replaced by southern Europeans, especially Greeks, Poles, Italians, Austrians, and Slavs . . . Southern Europeans are also used as deckhands on some boats.[1]

Mr. Hoagland's authority for these statements was the secretary of the Lake Carriers' Association.[2]

In listing the "most apparent causes back of the Slav and Magyar monopoly of the unskilled positions in the steel industry," Mr. Fitch includes, "the apparent fact that the steel companies have definitely sought this class of labor."[3] Subsequently, Mr. Fitch testified to the Stanley Committee, "I have reason to believe that this class of labor [foreign] is desired by the Steel Corporation for a number of reasons."[4] In following up this idea the committee devoted considerable attention to the following advertisement that appeared in the Pittsburgh papers on July 14, 1909, during the strike in the tin mills:

[1] Hoagland, *op. cit.*, p. 96.

[2] *Ibid.*, p. 93.

[3] Fitch, *op. cit.*, p. 143. Neither of these writers, it should be noted, imputed to the Corporation any attempt or desire to disregard the contract-labor law.

[4] *Stanley Hearings*, 1911, vol. iv, p. 2921.

Wanted—60 tin house men, tinners, catchers, and helpers to work in open shops, Syrians, Poles and Roumanians preferred; steady employment and good wages to men willing to work; fare paid and no fees charged for this work. Central Employment Bureau, 628 Penn. Avenue.[1]

From the testimony of Mr. W. A. Irvin, assistant to the vice-president of the American Sheet and Tin Plate Company, the Committee developed the fact that this company had engaged the Central Employment Bureau above mentioned to secure men during about five months beginning in July, 1909. Mr. Irvin further testified that when the manager of the employment bureau informed him that the supply of American labor had been exhausted by the needs of the hot mills, he gave to the manager a list of the foreigners preferred in the order of preference. Throughout the discussion Mr. Irvin and the Corporation's attorney, Mr. Reed, insisted that the advertisement meant that Syrians, Poles, and Roumanians were preferred to other types of foreigners, not to Americans; but it is evident that this interpretation has no support in the language actually used.[2] Questions from Mr. Beall of the Committee brought out the facts that prior to this strike of 1909 during which the above advertisement and others like it were inserted in Pittsburgh papers, the American Sheet and Tin Plate Company had dealt with unions, but that subsequent to it the company maintained an " open " shop.[3]

In the hearings before the Senate Committee that investigated the 1919 strike, charges were again made by labor officials that the Corporation had engaged foreign workmen with the deliberate intent of thereby smashing unions. The following interchange constitutes the official denial:

[1] *Stanley Hearings*, 1911, vol. iv, p. 3074.

[2] *Ibid.*, pp. 3059, 3061, 3062, 3071.

[3] *Ibid.*, pp. 3065, 3066.

The Chairman. Now the charge has been made here that your company had the policy of employing foreigners of different nationalities and putting them around in the different places so as to prevent any cohesive action among the men.

Mr. Gary. There is absolutely no foundation for that statement.[1]

The balancing of the evidence on this issue must be left to the reader's judgment.

Control of the press, charged against the Steel Corporation as it has been against numerous other concerns and against " big business " in general, is the second of the " alleged " methods of fighting labor organizations listed above. Evidence establishing the contention that the United States Steel Corporation directly or indirectly bribed or unduly influenced any newspaper has not come to light. The writer is inclined to believe that it does not exist. In making this statement, however, there is no intention of excusing the press for the part it almost invariably plays in labor disputes. Organized labor has rarely received a square deal from the newspapers and the truth of this statement has seldom, if ever, been so conclusively demonstrated as in the strike of 1919. There is no need of reproducing here the detailed facts presented in section two of *Public Opinion and the Steel Strike* on " The Pittsburgh Newspapers and the Strike ", but among other things the facts were there established that

1. The Pittsburgh newspapers failed to collect and publish the circumstances preceding the strike.

There were no general stories detailing the companies and mills in the industry, the numbers or characteristics of the workmen, their hours of labor, their wages, their living conditions, no history of the year's organizing campaign, no detailed lists

[1] *Senate Hearings*, 1919, p. 204.

of strikers' "demands," no summary of efforts to avert the strike. These things . . . were not " news " so far as the Pittsburgh newspapers were concerned.[1]

2. The point of view which dominated the news columns and editorials of the Pittsburgh papers was identical with that expressed in the numerous advertisements they carried which characterized the strike as " un-American ", " disloyal ", and " Bolshevistic ", and urged the men to return to work.[2]

3. The real grievances of the strikers on such matters as hours, housing and social conditions, the difficulty of bringing complaints to the attention of superiors, and similar matters were almost disregarded in the " news " published in Pittsburgh.[3]

4. Misleading and sometimes absolutely false headlines were regularly used to hide the facts when the preceding day's events happened to be favorable to the strikers.[4]

5. False stories calculated to break the morale of strikers were printed, such as the statement published in the *Gazette-Times* on December 5 that organizer T. J. Conboy had admitted defeat and quit Johnstown, and the statement published in the *Press* on the same date that the National Committee had called off the strike.[5]

Evidence is presented in the final section of this report to show that newspapers in other cities were, in spite of a number of exceptions, as unfair to organized labor as were the Pittsburgh papers.

[1] *Public Opinion and the Steel Strike*, p. 93.
[2] *Ibid.*, pp. 96-110.
[3] *Ibid.*, p. 111 *et seq.*
[4] *Ibid.*, pp. 114, 115, 134, 137, 138. Specific cases are discussed in detail on the pages cited.
[5] *Ibid.*, p. 139.

For an explanation of this situation recourse need not be had to the " purchase " of editors and reporters or " influence " exerted upon the advertising manager; a simple and sufficient reason is found in the fact that newspaper publishers and editors are by training and situation invested with the same habits of thought that persist among the majority of American business men. They do not have to be " bought " to express ideas they already hold. With the expression of such ideas in editorial columns there can be no quarrel—that is what editorial columns are for and one does not have to read them — but the vital difficulty is, of course, that the newspapers do not keep the anti-labor bias of their editors and publishers out of their news columns. As long as this condition exists there is no particular point in investigating charges that the Steel Corporation, or any other corporation, is fighting labor by controlling the press.

More serious in many respects than any of the matters heretofore considered is the charge that the Corporation has controlled public officials to the extent that civil liberties have been seriously interfered with. The degree to which this alleged situation exists varies widely from place to place, according to those who make the charges, but seems to be worst in western Pennsylvania. The specific counts in the indictment include the abrogation of the rights of freedom of speech and of assembly, the control of public officials, and intimidation and violence by state troopers and " special " peace officers. There is no space here for a recapitulation of the evidence which has been accumulating for many years. Nor does it seem possible to reach conclusions of a desirable definiteness from the evidence available. The very nature of the issues makes it certain that the same facts and circumstances will be reported differently by actual eyewitnesses; reported so differently in fact that the reader of the conflicting affidavits or testimony is prompted to ask himself whether it is possible that the accounts can be concerned with the same events. No clearer example can be found of the difficulties encountered than that of the murder of Mrs Fannie Snellings, an organizer for the United Mine Workers of America.

As presented from the strikers' point of view, Mrs. Snellings was "deliberately murdered" on August 26, 1919, after "open threats" had been made to "get" her because of her success in organizing both Corporation and independent workers in mines and steel mills. The immediate occasion was an attack by drunken deputy sheriffs led by a mine official on some pickets stationed at a mine of the Allegheny Coal and Coke Company (not connected with the Corporation) at West Natrona, Pennsylvania. Mrs. Snellings protested against the clubbing of a picket, Joseph Strzelecki, who was already on the ground fatally wounded by the fire of the deputies. She was knocked down by a blow from a club in the hands of the mine official and as she tried to drag herself away was killed by the deputies. In concluding the account the following statements were made:

Thus perished noble Fannie Sellins: shot in the back by so-called peace officers. . . . Many people witnessed this horrible murder. The guilty men were named openly in the newspapers and from a hundred platforms. Yet no one was ever punished for the crime. Witnesses were spirited away or intimidated, and the whole matter hushed up in true Steel Trust fashion.[1]

Mr. Fitzpatrick in testifying to the Senate Committee in 1919 made about the same statements except that according to him the woman's name was "Snellings", not "Sellins" as Foster has it, and the murder occurred at Brackenridge.[2]

[1] Foster, *op. cit.*, pp. 146-148.
[2] *Senate Hearings*, 1919, pp. 20-22.

Judge Gary later testified that the Corporation had no connection of any sort with the killing and quoted the testimony of Dr. G. L. Baumgartener at the coroner's inquest as follows: " I made a thorough examination of the body and I did not find a wound in the back." Other extracts from the testimony and verdict were introduced to show that the deputy sheriffs guarding the property of the Allegheny Coal and Coke Company were attacked; that there was a riot; that " There were no innocent bystanders. Therefore everyone in the crowd was guilty of rioting "; and that ". . . from the evidence and post-mortem examination made the jury find death was due to the above cause [gunshot wound in left temple] and the same was justifiable and in self-defense, and also recommend that Sheriff Haddock be commended in his prompt and successful action in protecting property and persons in that vicinity and the judgment exercised in the selection of his deputies." [1]

In reply to this the National Committee Organizing Iron and Steel Workers submitted an affidavit of two physicians of six and thirteen years' practice respectively who swore that in their examination of the woman's body " a gunshot wound was revealed entering in the left posterior scapular region about 2 inches to the left of the spinal column. . . ." [2] Thus it appears that from the pettiest detail of the exact spelling of the woman's name up to the most important point, the responsibility for the beginning of the incident, the groups of witnesses are agreed on nothing. Practically all the testimony was given under oath. On the basis of this sort of data it seems impossible to reach any conclusions. Other cases, such as the incident at North Clairton in which state troopers were charged with breaking up a strikers'

---

[1] *Senate Hearings*, 1919, pp. 147-150.
[2] *Ibid.*, p. 893.

meeting, knocking down and trampling on an American
flag, etc., and the incidents related by Father Kazincy of
state troopers' brutality, were entirely different affairs de-
pending upon who was telling the story,[1] and the opportunities for cross-examination of the witnesses.

On the other hand, many charges made by the labor group
were never answered and others answered inadequately.
The evidence on the Vandergrift and Apollo situation in
1909 as presented to the Stanley Committee two years later
indicates that United States Steel Corporation officials took
part in the mobbing of union organizers, ordered a hotel
proprietor to refuse accommodations to organizers on threat
of destroying the hotel, ordered Corporation employees to
cease patronizing the hotel, put pressure on the owner of a
vacant lot rented to the organizers so that he attempted to
cancel the agreement, and issued orders that any employee
seen entering the hall finally secured would be discharged.
The above statements of organizers were supported by statements from eleven individuals including the proprietor of
the hotel in question and the chief of police. The latter
deserves credit for refusing to be intimidated, but the bur-
gess was of an entirely different stripe.[2] In the 1919 strike
evidence of the abrogation of civil liberties came from so
many sources and in such quantities that it is impossible to
avoid the conclusion that a considerable part of it must be
true. Certainly there can be no question that some magis-
trates were quite careless in the matter of fining individuals
who were arrested on the charge of being " suspicious persons " and there is ample reason to believe that men who
were not working were much more likely to be fined despite

[1] *Cf. Senate Hearings,* 1919, pp. 548-550, 568, 569, with Interchurch,
Public Opinion and the Steel Strike, pp. 183-185; also Foster, *op. cit.,*
pp. 121, 122, with *Senate Hearings,* 1919, pp. 880-883.

[2] *Stanley Hearings,* 1911, vol. iv, 3142-3147.

one official denial.[1] Without doubt there was arbitrary and discriminatory use made by certain officials of their power to issue or refuse permits for public meetings. This situation seems to have been worst in Homestead, Braddock, Monessen, McKeesport, and Duquesne. In the last named place Mayor Crawford told J. G. Brown, organizer, that "Jesus Christ cannot come in and hold a meeting here in Duquesne."[2]

But from such a mass of contradictions and recriminations nothing appears clearly enough to justify the definite statement that the Corporation was or was not accessory to the abrogation of civil liberties as part of its anti-union fight. The impossibility of definiteness on that point, however, should not prevent us from remembering the evils inherent in a situation where an industrial organization either owns outright or dominates a civic unit. The evils have long been recognized and need only to be recalled. In the former case, existing at McDonald, Wilson Station, Chickasaw, and numerous coal towns operated by Corporation subsidiaries, there is no town government in the usual sense of the term; the functions usually performed by officials selected by the voters are directed by the employers of the town's residents. Moreover, the Corporation is also the landlord of its employees, and although this position may never be used unjustly, the temptations to abuses which it presents are obvious. In other towns not owned by the Corporation it is the chief taxpayer, gives employment directly to the bulk of the male population, and by the concentration of its own working force indirectly gives employment to the various butchers, bakers, and candlestick makers

[1] *Cf. Senate Hearings,* 1919 pp. 576, 578, 590, and 685.
[2] *Public Opinion and the Steel Strike,* p. 171. For affidavits and statements covering the facts in these towns see pp. 179-181; 188-189; 191-198; 200-207.

who meet the needs of the steel workers. Inevitably this latter group feels that its prosperity is definitely dependent upon the continuous operation of the mills, and hence looks askance upon any development that may even temporarily hinder such continuous operation. To this must be added the fact that a very large percentage of steel employees are immigrants and that a large proportion of them have not been naturalized. Consequently, the bulk of the voters come from groups inclined to be favorable toward the Corporation, and these elect officials who have much the same habits of thought that they themselves have. In this manner we come to somewhat the same conclusion as that reached on newspaper men: public officials do not have to be "bought" for the reason that their training and preconceptions prompt them to act in a manner that redounds to the advantage of the Corporation, or of other employers. To lay the responsibility directly to 71 Broadway is unwarranted. A closer approximation to the truth is to consider the Corporation in this respect the beneficiary of a situation that predisposes mayors, burgesses, and other officials to take strong measures against the labor " agitator ".

Finally, it has been charged that certain features of the Corporation's so-called " welfare program " are actually little more than insidious methods to prevent the growth of a union spirit. The validity of such charges cannot be determined without a knowledge of this program, which is the subject of the following two chapters.

CHAPTER V

WELFARE

THE term welfare may include a great many items. In the following discussion the definition of the United States Bureau of Labor Statistics in its bulletin number 250 has been followed. There, welfare is defined as "anything for the comfort and improvement, intellectual or social, of the employees, over and above wages paid, which is not a necessity of the industry nor required by law."

The welfare program of the United States Steel Corporation can best be visualized by first making a rapid survey of its historical development and organization and then proceeding to an examination of its operation. As will be brought out later, individual items in the welfare program were receiving attention in various subsidiaries even before they became parts of the United States Steel Corporation, but the first general action taken was announced in an open letter of December 31, 1902—the inauguration of a stock subscription plan. The first stock was actually sold to the employees in January, 1903, and has continued to be sold in the first months of every year except 1915.

But this stock subscription plan has always remained more or less a thing apart, having little connection with the rest of the program. The real center, the source from which practically everything else has sprung, is the safety movement. Prior to the centralized efforts taken to lessen the frequency and severity of industrial accidents in the Corporation plants, each subsidiary had a casualty manager and handled its accidents as it saw fit, but in May, 1906, these men were all called together to settle on a more uniform system and to aid each other in every way possible. These meetings continued at irregular intervals until April, 1908, when a permanent committee on safety was appointed. Although this committee has always had one representative of the Corporation, the representatives of the larger subsidiaries have grown from five in 1908 to seven in 1911 and then to nine in 1918. The functions of this central committee as set forth in its *Bulletin Number Two* of July 1, 1911, are as follows:

(1) The Committee conducts thorough inspections of all plants of all subsidiary companies from the standpoint of safety. These inspections are in addition to those made by the companies themselves and are conducted by inspectors selected from companies other than those operating the plants in question. The inspectors report and are responsible to the Safety Committee and not to the companies whose plants are under inspection. From time to time and whenever special circumstances seem to require such action, the Committee, or various members thereof, make these inspections themselves.

(2) The Committee acts as a clearing house for all information relating to the safety of employees. All safety devices and other methods of increasing the safety of the workmen and of interesting the men in their own safety and that of their fellow workmen are reported to the Committee by the subsidiary companies in which they originate. These safety methods and devices are carefully considered by the Committee and if approved are recommended to all the subsidiary companies, often with improvements suggested by the Committee. In this manner descriptions with full details, photographs, diagrams and complete information of all matters dealing with the safety of employees is disseminated among the subsidiary companies.

(3) The Committee at its quarterly meetings considers all serious accidents which have occurred in any of the companies

during the preceding quarter, with a view to devising means for preventing the recurrence of similar accidents.

In addition to this committee on safety of the Corporation each subsidiary maintains what is designated as a "central safety committee" composed of important officials from each of the plants, mines, railroad divisions, or whatever industrial units constitute the corporation in question. It meets monthly and performs duties similar to those of the safety committee of the Corporation. In companies where there is no organization on sanitation the duties of the various safety committees have been extended to cover that work. Subordinate to the central safety committee are the "plant safety committees" made up of important officials in an individual plant. Such committees meet monthly, weekly, or in some cases daily, and make inspections of the plants at regular intervals. Each plant also has a "workmen's safety committee" consisting usually of three men from the rank and file of the mill. It meets monthly, or in some cases weekly, makes regular inspections of the plant, investigates accidents that have occurred, and recommends means of preventing similar accidents. Its members are changed periodically so that each man in the plant will serve on the committee. In addition, some plants maintain "department and special committees" composed of foremen, master mechanics, and skilled workmen. These committees meet at irregular intervals, make investigations of the plant, and conduct special investigations of particular problems. All of the committees in the subsidiaries were "organized shortly after [the] Steel Corporation Safety Committee." [1]

By the time the hierarchy of committees outlined above had become an accomplished fact the Corporation announced

[1] United States Steel Corporation Bureau of Safety, Relief, Sanitation, and Welfare, *Bulletin Number Four* (New York, 1913), pp. 3-4.

a new feature of its safety campaign. Everything possible was being done to limit the number and seriousness of accidents, but since it was deemed impossible to eliminate them, steps were now taken to afford the men, or their dependents, some accident relief. The " Voluntary Accident Relief Plan " went into operation on May 1, 1910, but has since been largely superseded by workmen's compensation laws.

In the same year the Corporation announced another project which would go into effect on January 1, 1911: the pension system. At the time he retired from the steel industry Mr. Carnegie had created a fund of $4,000,000, the income from which was to be used in paying pensions to superannuated employees and benefits for serious or fatal accidents. This relief fund had apparently been quite distinct from the Carnegie Steel Company, a personal gift from Mr. Carnegie. In his own words it was " an acknowledgment of the deep debt which I owe to the workmen who have contributed so greatly to my success." [2] In 1910, however, it became definitely a Corporation affair, for in that year the fund was increased to $12,000,000, the additional $8,000,000 payable in installments; the accident relief features of the Carnegie plan were abolished; and the benefits of the new " United States Steel and Carnegie Pension Fund " extended to all employees of the Corporation.

By this time it had become evident that a committee of safety meeting only at somewhat lengthy intervals did not provide sufficient coordination and centralization for the rapidly expanding work. For this reason a central office in that of the Corporation at 71 Broadway, New York City, was established. This was at first called the Bureau of Safety, Relief, Sanitation, and Welfare, but with the growth of statutory enactments concerning relief that feature of the work became much less a Corporation matter, and the word

---

[1] Quoted in Fitch, *op. cit.*, p. 195.

was dropped from the Bureau's name, so that it is now the Bureau of Safety, Sanitation, and Welfare. The original manager, Mr. C. L. Close, is still in charge of the Bureau and devotes all his time to the work. The scope of operations of the Bureau is perhaps best expressed in its *Bulletin Number Four* of November, 1913.

This Bureau acts as a central station in obtaining information and disseminating it among the subsidiary companies. It carries on the administrative work of both the Committee of Safety and the Committee on Sanitation. It distributes to the subsidiary companies comparative statements on accident prevention, compiled from reports sent in by them periodically, so that they may benefit by each others' experience. The Bureau is constantly in communication with municipal, state, and national authorities, with other employers of labor, and with various persons engaged or interested in this work . . . it keeps the subsidiary companies informed of the latest and best methods in accident prevention and welfare work.

The sanitation committee mentioned above was established in October, 1911, with five members: a chairman from the Corporation and the presidents of four subsidiaries. The membership was reduced to four some years ago by the death of one of the subsidiary representatives. Its work is similar to that of the safety committee—the collection and dissemination of information. It is aided in this by a sub-committee composed of one representative from each subsidiary, most of them sanitary engineers, and by the sanitation (or safety) committees of the various plants.

During the next eight years no changes in organization were made. The Bureau and the various committees mentioned continued to follow the plans established, the most marked tendency being that of the Bureau to extend its advisory and informational functions over a wider and wider field. On September 4, 1919, the organization was completed with the formation of the Committee on Housing. This group is composed of twelve men, each representing one of the larger subsidiary companies. It " meets periodically to consider all phases of the housing problem, including town planning, design and construction of comfortable houses for employees." [1]

The central feature of the Corporation's welfare work has always been the safety movement. Interest was first aroused there and it has remained probably the most important, well-organized, and effective of the Corporation's activities, though the expenditures for other items are now greater. Since the organization of the work under numerous committees has been explained and their functions pointed out, the next topic for consideration is accident prevention.

In attempting to prevent accidents the Corporation has maintained that the two essential elements in a safety campaign are: (1) teach the workmen to be more careful, (2) make all machinery, tools, etc., as nearly fool-proof, and hence as nearly accident-proof, as possible. Mr. Close, manager of the Bureau of Safety, Sanitation, and Welfare, believes that seventy to eighty per cent of all accidents are attributable to thoughtlessness or carelessness either on the part of the workman himself or on the part of his fellow workmen.[2] One of the bulletins issued by his Bureau since he took charge goes further and says that the workers are solely or partially responsible in ninety per cent of the cases.[3]

[1] U. S. Steel Corporation, Bureau of Safety, *Bulletin Number Eight* (New York, 1920), p. 7.

[2] Close, C. L., *Welfare Work in the Steel Industry, an Address at the Annual Meeting of the American Iron and Steel Institute* (New York, 1920), p. 8.

[3] U. S. Steel Corporation, Bureau of Safety, *Bulletin Number Eight*, p. 13. It is interesting to note the evidence collected on this point by Miss Crystal Eastman, author of the volume on *Work-Accidents and*

The educational work of the Corporation on an employee
concerning safety begins before the man is actually employed.
In many plants as he enters the gate of the mill a large sign,
illuminated by night, warns him that " the prevention of accidents and injuries, by all possible means, is a personal duty
which *Everyone* owes not to himself alone but also to his
fellow workers." In the employment office he finds another sign printed in seven languages, with a list of forty
" safety precepts." These are prefaced by the following
statement: " To men seeking employment: Unless you are
willing to be careful to avoid injury to yourself and fellow-
workmen do not ask for employment. We do not want
careless men in our employ." [1]   Wherever he turns there are

the Law, in the Pittsburgh Survey of the Russell Sage Foundation.
Chapter six of her book is an analysis of 410 work-accident fatalities
in the Pittsburgh district, all industries being included. The results of
her analysis showed that 28 per cent of the fatalities were " unavoidable," that 32 per cent of the fatalities were solely or partly the fault of
the worker. These 410 deaths were caused by 377 accidents. In these
the " causes attributed solely to

employers or those who represent them in positions of authority 29.97%
those killed or their fellow workmen 27.85%
both of the above 15.91%
neither of above .... 26.27% "

(Eastman, C., *Work-Accidents and the Law* [New York, 1901], p. 103.)
    In discussing this matter of the responsibility for accident, the U. S.
Commissioner of Labor in his report to the Senate in 1911 stated that " the
assignment of the responsibility for accidents is largely a matter of
judgment." In his report were analyzed 7,750 cases of disabling accidents occurring in one large steel plant in the six years ending December 31, 1910. The results may be expressed as follows:

> " Hazard of the industry 60%
> Negligence of worker 7%
> Negligence of fellow-worker 6%
> Negligence of employer 4%
> Not disclosed by the record ..... 23% "

(Neill, *op. cit.,* vol. iv, p. 172-174.)
    [1] U. S. Steel Corporation, Bureau of Safety, *Bulletin Number Three*
(New York, 1912), p. 48.

signs warning him of danger or of the necessity for ever-
lasting carefulness. The Corporation has adopted a red
ball or circle as a danger signal and hopes to make it as
universally recognized as the Red Cross. In addition to
thousands of these red balls the ordinary " Danger," " Look
out for the cars," skull and cross bones, etc., etc., signs are
numerous. Through the plants of the various subsidiaries
there are more than 2000 bulletin boards of safety. On these
are posted clippings of notices of accidents, safety propaganda, pictures of goggles whose cracked or broken lenses
show what might have happened to the workmen had they not
been worn, rules for piling brick, for piling sacks of cement,
for piling iron rods, in fact, everything conceivably connected
with accidents and their prevention. Another type of bulletin
board shows two complete sets of tools, one in perfect order,
the other bent, chipped, dull, or otherwise unfit for service.
The workers are notified that the continued use of imperfect
tools is a challenge to disaster. The sign idea is even
carried into the homes of the employees by printing and dis-
tributing calendars bearing safety notices. A singularly
efficacious means of attracting the worker's attention to a
safety precept is to print it on his pay envelope or enclose it
with his pay. Foreigners who can read no English lose no
time in having the message translated. Many of the plants
publish papers or periodicals of some kind which almost invariably contain some news of the safety movement.

No small part of the safety campaign is concentrated in
the use of moving pictures, made in and around company
plants, and shown to workmen as a part of a free entertain-
ment which includes other pictures. The pictures are : " An
American in the Making," taken in 1912, " The Reason
Why " in 1917, and " Why " in 1918. The first combines
an illustration of safety devices with the rise of " an ignorant
Hungarian peasant " from penury to a good job in one of

the Corporation's mills. The others are purely safety propaganda showing the right and wrong way to use tools, make repairs, perform various tasks, and more or less lurid representations of bandaged, one-eyed, one-legged individuals who failed to exercise the proper care. Records kept by the Corporation at playgrounds and auditoriums where these pictures have been used show that they are well attended.

In addition to this educational work a great deal of emphasis is laid on the prevention of accidents by the use of safety appliances. An attempt even to list the devices used would make a fair sized pamphlet. Several of the bulletins of the Corporation's Bureau of Safety contain cuts of these devices, and in one of them are several pages of drawings and specifications, which would enable anyone to adopt and use the same precautions. Moreover, the committee of safety prepared in September, 1912, a set of *General Requirements for Safety pertaining to Physical Conditions.* These requirements, as amended in 1918, are issued in a pamphlet of sixty-four pages and are distributed to any interested outsiders as well as to all subsidiaries. The recommendations of the committee are briefly stated on hundreds of matters, among which may be mentioned: ventilation in benzol plants; the construction of a metal closet lined with asbestos on cranes to give protection to the craneman in case anything goes wrong with the machinery when hoisting hot metal; the installation of automatic valves to prevent gas from getting back into engines; the equipment of all electric traveling cranes with substantial fenders or plate guards extending to below top of rail and projecting in front of all bridge and trolley track wheels, such fenders being rigidly attached to the carriage or end frame and of a shape and form that will tend to push and raise a man's hand, arm, or leg off the rail and away from the wheel; the installation of spark arresters on all emery wheels, of shields on all circular and band-saws, jointers, planers, etc., and of hooped-in safety cages on all ladders.

A somewhat unique safety precaution has been adopted in most of the Corporation's plants, first, perhaps, in those of the American Steel and Wire Company. Power in these plants is furnished largely by steam engines. Each engine is equipped with a safety stop valve which shuts the engine down automatically when it exceeds a certain safe speed. The valve may also be operated by pushing any one of a number of electric buttons located throughout the mill, each marked by a small blue light. In case a workman becomes caught in the machinery or there is a breakdown of any sort, the buttons make it easy to cut off the steam and stop the engine. A system of this sort is, of course, of little or no value unless kept in perfect working order, and hence the company has arranged that the daily shutting-down of the engines shall be by means of these buttons, and that once a week each button shall be pushed with a man at the engine throttle to see that it works properly.

In departments driven by electricity there are motor stops corresponding to the automatic engine stops just described. In some cases these are controlled by push buttons and in others a rope is carried directly from the machinery to the switch controlling the motor, so that the switch can be pulled by means of the rope in emergencies.[1]

But the vital point is not to be found in a list of the measures taken to prevent accidents; it lies in the extent to which the safety movement is a success, and first, in the success of the educational campaign. There is no doubt that for many years the attitude of the workmen and the foremen in the steel mills and in the mines was one largely flavored by recklessness. They seemed to think that the careful man was somewhat of a coward or a mollycoddle.

[1] Eastman, *op. cit.,* pp. 255-6.

The amount of change in this respect is, of course, largely a matter of opinion, but most of the officials of the various companies seem to believe that the change has been very pronounced, that the men are not only careful of their own lives but of the lives of others.[1]

A more acceptable indication of the progress made is to be found in the statistics of accidents in the Corporation's plants. The bulletins of the Corporation's Bureau of Safety have presented in each issue a bar diagram showing the " per cent decrease in accident rate under 1906 per 1,000 employees " for every year since 1906 with a calculation of the number of men considered to have been saved from serious accident. The facts are presented in the following table.

TABLE XII

PERCENTAGE DECREASE IN ACCIDENT RATE BELOW 1906 RATE AND NUMBER ESTIMATED TO HAVE BEEN SAVED FROM ACCIDENT, U. S. STEEL CORPORATION, 1907-1923

Year	Per cent decrease in accident rate below 1906	Number saved from accident	Year	Per cent decrease in accident rate below 1906	Number saved from accident
1907....	10.40	532	1916....	31.60	1,957
1908....	18.21	783	1917....	41.63	2,891
1909....	25.28	1,236	1918....	46.84	3,094
1910....	43.49	2,215	1919....	46.84	2,944
1911....	41.26	2,012	1920...	53.90	3,817
1912....	36.06	2,023	1921....	53.16	2,676
1913....	38.29	2,273	1922....	56.88	3,234
1914....	40.52	1,748	1923....	55.40	3,798
1915....	43.54	2,145			

The actual figures on accidents and the rates from which

[1] *Cf.* Bureau of Safety, *Bulletin Number Two* (New York, 1911), p. 4; *Survey*, vol. 24, p. 205, an article by D. S. Beyer, chief safety inspector of the American Steel and Wire Co.; Bureau of Safety, *Bulletin Number Six* (New York, 1921 [third edition]), p. 21.

these decreases have been computed have never been made public by the Corporation.[1]

But accepting the figures given as accurate they are still inadequate to give a complete comprehension of the accident situation. The Corporation's figures cover the frequency rates of " serious " accidents, with no explanation as to what " serious " means. Thus the severity of the accidents, in the sense of the number of days lost, is left out of consideration. The importance of the severity rate in determining the true condition and the erroneous conclusions likely to be reached by the use of a frequency rate or a severity rate alone can not be discussed here. For my purpose it is sufficient to note that after examining the records of a large

[1] In *Public Opinion and the Steel Strike* (p. 257), issued by the Commission of Inquiry of the Interchurch World Movement, are presented some figures on the results achieved by the Corporation in reducing accidents. These figures, as far as can be ascertained from the text which accompanies them, are intended to represent the frequency rates per 1,000 300-day workers and severity rates per 1,000 300-day workers for the whole Corporation,—in detail from 1906 to 1913, a general average for the period 1914 to 1919. But with only one minor variation these figures correspond in all items with two tables presented in Neill's 1911 *Report on the Conditions of Employment in the Iron and Steel Industry of the United States* (vol. iv, p. 115) and United States Bureau of Labor Statistics bulletin number 234 on *The Safety Movement in the Iron and Steel Industry from 1907 to 1917* (p. 15). Neill's table covers the period 1900 to 1911 inclusive and the Bureau's the period 1905 to 1917 inclusive. The difficulty lies in the fact that both the government tables are given " for one large plant which has done considerable safety work." A comparison of the three tables makes the conclusion inevitable that they all represent the accident experience of the same plant, and internal evidence in the government publications makes it fairly certain that the " one large plant " was a part of the Corporation; but since this plant never had more than 10,852 300-day workers, whereas the Corporation was employing from 150,000 to 250,000 persons at the time, I am inclined to doubt the validity of the sample. This doubt is strengthened by the application of the Corporation's method of figuring the accident rate as a decrease below the 1906 rate as a base. The computation shows that this plant made a much better record than the Corporation as a whole claims for itself.

group of steel mills for the years 1914 to 1919, Mr. Lucian W. Chaney came to the following conclusions:

"(1) Anything like a satisfactory understanding of an accident condition is impossible without the use of severity rates.

(2) The methods which satisfactorily control minor injury will not suffice for the control of death causes." [1]

Another method of gauging the success of the campaign is to note the changes in the ratings by insurance companies of the men employed in the mills. These changes between 1908 and 1919 are reflected in the following table of the rates of the Prudential Insurance Company. There are five premium charges: regular, special, intermediate, medium, and hazardous rates. The figures quoted are for a whole life policy at age thirty-five.[2]

Thus of the eleven occupations or occupation groups listed, eight were classed as hazardous in 1908, none in 1919. Of these eight, four had dropped one rank in degree of danger, three had dropped two ranks, and one had passed completely out of the extra-charge group and was accepted at regular premium charges. This is indeed a remarkable showing.

In concluding this section on accident prevention it is no more than fair to state that the Corporation's efforts are probably unequalled by any other large industrial concern in this country. It has devoted a great deal of thought and energy and a great many dollars to making its plants more safe for its men. The results achieved it may well be proud of, and for them it certainly deserves great credit.

[1] "War-Time Trend of Employment and Accidents in a Group of Steel Mills," *Monthly Labor Review*, vol. ix, pp. 222-232 (1210)-(1220) (Oct., 1919). It is interesting to observe that Mr. Chaney puts the responsibility for this failure to hold down the death rate upon the shoulders of the safety engineers, p. 231 (1219).

[2] *Senate Hearings*, 1919, p. 188. The statement made here that there are only four premium charges is incorrect.

TABLE XIII

INSURANCE RATINGS, 1908 AND 1919, OF SELECTED OCCUPATIONS
IN STEEL MILLS

Department and Occupation	1908	1919
Blast furnace:		
Blower	13.22*	†
Keeper	13.22*	2.77‡
Stove tenders, gas washers, keeper's helpers,		
cinder snapper, tuyere man, water tender....	12.22*	5.67§
Bessemer plant:		
Cupola melter, liner, vessel man, ladle man,		
stopper setter	13.22*	5.67§
Blowers and regulators	2.96‡	2.77‡
Open hearth plant:		
Melter	13.22*	2.27‡
Melter's first, second, third helpers	13.22*	5.67§
Crucible steel plant:		
Melter..................................	13.22*	2.77‡
Pot filler, shaker, pourer, moulder, lifter	13.22*	5.67§
Rolling mills:		
Roller..................................	2.96‡	†
Soaking pit heater	5.92‖	2.77‡

* Hazardous.   † Regular.   ‡ Special.   § Medium.   ‖ Intermediate.

Since it is apparently impossible to prevent all accidents,
the Corporation endeavors to take care of the victims of
those accidents which it has failed to prevent, the first method
being the first aid and rescue activities. The following
facts are summarized from *Bulletin Number Four* of the
Bureau of Safety, Sanitation and Welfare, issued in November, 1913. With some variations it will apply to all companies.

All of the mining companies and many of the manufacturing companies of the Corporation have first aid and
rescue crews composed of employees specially trained for
the work. This work is purely voluntary on the part of the
men who engage in it, but each man has to have a physician's
statement certifying that he is physically fit for the training
and the subsequent work. First aid crews are composed

of from four to six men who meet periodically for training by the company doctor in a course of about twelve lessons made up of lectures, demonstrations, and drills. The work goes on continually, fresh crews being turned out all the time, and certificates are given at the satisfactory completion of the course. The primary purposes of these first aid crews are to provide an aseptic or sterile dressing for the injury and to see that the injured man reaches home or a hospital safely. Rescue crews are composed of from five to eight men. Their training consists in the actual use of a helmet or other breathing apparatus while doing such work as would be necessary in rescuing workmen from a mine or building filled with smoke or noxious gases. Equipment for the men consists of helmet, storage battery light, oxygen cylinder, and the usual tools required for the work. On January 1, 1924, 20,719 men had been trained in first aid and rescue work, and 863 were in training at the 66 stations maintained by the Corporation.

In the larger plants of the Corporation first aid rooms and dressing stations are scattered over the works. These handle only the most trivial accidents. For injuries requiring more skilled care or perhaps better equipment there are one or more emergency hospitals operated according to the standard specifications laid down by the particular subsidiary, but all more or less uniform.

The standard emergency hospitals of the Carnegie Steel Company are forty-six feet and three inches by thirty-two feet and nine inches outside measurements, of steel and concrete fireproof construction, and have the following rooms: waiting room, re-dressing room, operating room, ward room (3 beds) bathroom, and nurse's room on the main floor, and x-ray room, laboratory, and morgue in the basement. The staff of such a hospital consists of one doctor, three graduate female nurses, one male nurse, one stenographer, one clerk, and a janitress. The equipment is modern in every particular. The stations are able to handle from 350 to 400 cases a day.[1]

For cases in which the patient is likely to be confined for more than a day the Corporation utilizes its own base hospitals or, more commonly, local hospitals operated privately or by the municipality. Of the base hospitals built and operated by one of the companies, those at Fairfield, Alabama; Gary, Indiana; Lynch, Kentucky; and Hibbing, Minnesota, are probably the best. Lack of space forbids any detailed description of them but the cuts, plans, statement of equipment, etc. in the Corporation's bulletins, reinforced by the testimony of former employees of the Corporation, give assurance that they are first class in every respect. The employees of the Corporation are treated at these hospitals without any charge in cases of accidents. In cases of ordinary sickness the workman or any member of his family will receive attention at rates which are, according to the Bureau, extremely moderate. On January 1, 1924, there were 13 base hospitals and 389 emergency stations, large and small, in the various subsidiaries of the Corporation.

Following up the accident prevention and the first aid work is the Voluntary Accident Relief scheme. This need not delay us long since it has been almost completely superseded by workmen's compensation laws in the various states. The Corporation claims that its plan " went into operation May 1, 1910, before any such laws had been enacted in the United States." [2] This statement is not quite accurate, for

[1] U. S. Bureau of Labor Statistics, Bulletin No. 250, *Welfare Work in Industrial Establishments* (Washington, 1919), pp. 21 *et seq.* A complete list of the equipment is given in the bulletin.

[2] U. S. Steel Corporation, Bureau of Safety, *Bulletin Number Three*, p. 4.

Maryland passed such a law in 1902, declared unconstitutional in 1904; and Montana passed a law on March 4, 1910, effective October 1, 1910, which was also declared unconstitutional. Had the Corporation stated that its plan became operative before any constitutionally perfect state enactment, it would have been correct. Of the state laws subsequently upheld as constitutional that of Wisconsin was the first to become effective, May 3, 1911,[1] almost exactly a year after the Corporation's plan went into effect.

The following summary of the relief plan is quoted from the Bureau of Safety's *Bulletin Nnmber Three* (p. 4):

Relief is paid, regardless of legal liability and without any legal proceedings. Even application for relief is not required.

The Companies provide treatment by surgeons and hospitals.

No relief is paid for the first ten days of disability, such restriction having been found necessary in all legislation on the subject.

Temporary Disability—Single men: 35 per cent of wages up to fifty-two weeks; 2 per cent added for each additional year of service over five years; maximum, $1.50 per day. Married men: 50 per cent of wages up to fifty-two weeks; 2 per cent added for each additional year of service over five years; 5 per cent added for each child under sixteen years of age; maximum $2.50 per day.

Permanent Disability—Loss of hand, twelve months' wages; arm, eighteen months' wages; foot, nine months' wages; leg, twelve months' wages; eye, six months' wages.

Permanent Total Disability—Such an amount as shall be required to make suitable provisions for the injured man, but in no case less than the death relief.

Death—Funeral expenses, not to exceed $100.00. Married men: Eighteen months' wages; 3 per cent added for each year

[1] U. S. Bureau of Labor Statistics, Bulletin No. 272, *Workmen's Compensation Legislation in the United States and Canada, 1919* (Washington, 1921), p. 13.

of service over five years; 10 per cent added for each child under sixteen years of age; maximum, $3,000.

Though the Corporation is entitled to a great deal of credit for establishing this relief plan, it should not be forgotten that the subject of accident compensation had been for several years very much before the public eye, that state commissions all over the country were busy drafting laws at this time, and that a total of eleven states actually passed laws in 1911.

CHAPTER VI

WELFARE (*Continued*)

THE second main division of the Corporation's welfare program may be designated as "Community Health Work," under which are included sanitation, medical services, restaurants, and housing.

As stated in the discussion of the historical development of this work, the sanitation committee was created in October, 1911, only a few months after the organization of the Bureau of Safety, Sanitation and Welfare. This committee first turned its attention to the question of water supply and the disposition of fecal matter. Under its direction each subsidiary company had analyses made of all water used for drinking purposes, a total of about 2,300 analyses being made. In cases where sources were found impure they were abandoned. Regular analyses are now made of all water at least once a year and additional analyses whenever there is any suspicion that the water has become contaminated. In mining towns where springs and wells are used, extra precautions are taken to avoid pollution by surface water or otherwise.[1]

But if these precautions are taken in securing a pure supply, no less energy must be spent in making sure that it remains so. Twenty years ago the bucket and dipper, the cask, and the common cups were as prevalent in the steel industry as they were elsewhere, but by January 1, 1924, the

[1] U. S. Steel Corporation, Bureau of Safety, *Bulletin Number Four,* p. 26.

various subsidiaries had installed 4,437 sanitary drinking fountains. A study of the pictures of these fountains in successive bulletins reveals the progress that has been made, and, incidentally, some of the troubles of a sanitary engineer. The first fixtures were of such a type that the user could put his mouth on or over the water outlet. Before long a sort of collar was put on them so that this practice was no longer possible. But in 1917 studies made at the University of Minnesota and published in the Public Health Reports of that state demonstrated that most so-called sanitary fountains were not so at all because of construction which permitted the water to fall back from the lips of the user on the outlet. The importance of this defect was emphasized in later publications of the Federal government.[1] Consequently the Corporation found itself with a good many hundreds of dollars invested in " sanitary " fountains which were not. However, it was determined not to lag behind and the " angle jet " fountain has been made the standard.

The temperature of the drinking water has received attention and in the majority of the plants is so regulated that it will be cool without being too cold. The best system probably is that of the National Tube Company. Water is kept circulating through the line at all times and is taken directly from the line so that there are no dead ends in which it may stand.

The second item on the program, the disposition of fecal matter, was, of course, particularly urgent in new towns or in old ones in which there was no sewage system. Even in localities with a sewage system the flush-range type of closets was used more or less extensively before the organization of the sanitation committee. These the committee characterized as " unsanitary, disagreeable, and objectionable ".[2] The

---

[1] U. S. Bureau of Labor Statistics, Bulletin No. 250, p. 40.

[2] U. S. Steel Corporation, Sanitation Committee, *General Requirements for Sanitary Installations* (New York, 1916), p. 16.

committee recommends that " closets should be of the individual bowl type with individual water seal and should be made of porcelain or vitreous china and not of enameled iron." [1]   The general adoption of this recommendation has done a great deal to improve conditions in the plants, though in some places the old type still persists.

The problem of the no-sewage town the Corporation has to a great measure solved in the company towns, where it has built privies of standard construction, well ventilated, fly-proof, and equipped with water-tight cans which render soil pollution impossible. At regular intervals the cans are replaced with others by a company sanitary man, conveyed to a septic tank or incinerator, and the contents disposed of. [2]

Another matter to which the sanitation committee has given considerable attention is the provision of adequate washroom and locker facilities. The question of individual wash basins has apparently given it some trouble, for it recommended as far back as 1911 that they be abolished and that goose-necked faucets high enough above a no-stopper trough to permit a man to get his head and shoulders under them comfortably be installed. Many of the companies already had long rows of beautiful white individual basins, but recent bulletins show that they are converting them into the high faucet flowing-stream type. The men use these facilities on their own time except in a few cases where a lead process is used and in which company time for washing is required by law.

Clothing lockers, too, have been the cause of no little discussion. The days are not so long past when there was no place for the miner or the mill-worker to change his clothes at the work; he was compelled to go home in his

[1] U. S. Steel Corporation, Sanitation Committee, *General Requirements for Sanitary Installations*, p. 16.

[2] U. S. Steel Corporation, Bureau of Safety, *Bulletin Number Four,* p. 26.

filth. Indeed this is still true to some extent but it is being
rapidly remedied. Lockers providing adequate space for the
clothing and permitting proper ventilation required an enormous amount of space. Moreover, it was highly desirable
that each man should have two lockers, one for his clean
street clothes while at work, another for his dirty mill clothes
overnight. This doubled the problem. Many of the subsidiaries believe they have solved it, however, with a system
of chains and pulleys which enable each man to swing his
clothes up well above the floor where they receive the maximum amount of ventilation but are not in contact with other
clothing. The lower end of the chain or wire is held by a
weight which is locked in place. In this way the system is
made as safe as one of lockers.

Other more or less miscellaneous matters which cannot be
treated in detail include the following: the abolition of the
common towel from the mines and plants; the provision in
company towns of a garbage can and a trash can for each
house and the regular removal of the contents by a company
employee; proper ventilation and lighting in all buildings
put up by the Corporation whether they are mills or resi-
dences; the prevention of malaria by draining swamps and
oiling pools where draining was not feasible—a work which
reduced the malaria rate in one Alabama town almost mirac-
ulously; the extermination of flies through campaigns of
education among the workmen and by setting an example in
company buildings; the installation of shavings and sawdust
removal systems in wood-working shops and of dust removal in the portland cement works; and the perfection and
use in some plants of refrigerating systems which pump
cool air through the works — particularly to those departments where the work is hottest.

The second feature of the community health work may
be termed medical services. The extent to which the com-

pany hospitals serve the workers has been indicated. Another item of importance is the work of the visiting or neighborhood nurses.

These visiting nurses were originally employed almost altogether by the mining companies, but since the scheme was so successful many of the manufacturing plants now utilize them. Their services are offered by the Corporation free to the employees but are not forced upon them. The chief duties of the nurses are to attend the sick; to give instruction and advice in matters of household sanitation, the economical purchasing of home necessities, and the care of children, especially infants; to conduct day nurseries in which the children of widows are cared for while they are at work; and, in general, to act as a counsellor, helper, and friend. These duties obviously require a union of technical knowledge with a pleasing and tactful personality. On January 1, 1924, there were 71 of these nurses in the employ of the Corporation's subsidiaries.

The final section of the medical services is the dental clinics, inaugurated by the Tennessee Coal, Iron and Railroad Company in the fall of 1915 with the employment of a dentist to care for the teeth of the children in the various schools maintained in whole or in part by the Company. The success of the work and the evident need for it encouraged its expansion, and in December, 1916, a permanent dental clinic with modern high-class equipment was established at the Fairfield (Alabama) medical dispensary. At first this clinic limited its work to the treatment of accidents and injuries received at work. Later the clinics took over the school work formerly done by a traveling dentist and opened their offices to all employees of the Company and their families. A dentist is employed in each office on a monthly salary. The charges made at these clinics average fifty per cent less than those of city dentists, according to the Bureau of Safety, Sanitation and Welfare. In September, 1917, similar clinics were established at Docena, Edgewater, and Bayview; in March, 1918, at Wenonah; in June, 1918, at Ishkooda; and on November 1, 1918, at Johns and at Ensley. The Bureau notes that the employees no longer have to make long trips from the mining camps to the city for dental work and that hence " much time is saved to the company ".

A feature of the dental work is the " tooth-brush drill " at the schools. Every pupil is required to purchase a tooth brush and cup and the work of the day begins with a fifteen minute period devoted to a vigorous washing of teeth and some mild setting-up exercises.[1]

The results accomplished appear to be very good. On the whole, however, it seems that the strict salary basis on which the dentists are paid is not conducive to the highest efficiency.

The next part of the health work to be considered is the company restaurant. The investigations of the Bureau of Labor Statistics in 1916 and 1917 published in its bulletin number 250 on *Welfare Work for Employees in Industrial Establishments in the United States* show that "Of the industries reporting restaurants the iron and steel industry and foundries and machine shops show the smallest proportion of these facilities for the general working force. Their restaurants are mainly for the office force and for officials . . ." (p. 53).

The testimony of the official of the Corporation with whom I talked would indicate that he does not think this criticism quite fair when applied to the Corporation alone. He explained that there were separate rooms, sometimes separate restaurants, for the superintendents and foremen

[1] U. S. Steel Corporation, Bureau of Safety, *Bulletin Number Seven* (New York, 1918), pp. 36-37.

because the plants made a practice of having these men get together once each day to talk over matters in the plant, and the lunch time was the most convenient. On his own statement, however, the Corporation records show only some 16,000 men regular patrons of the company restaurants. As I understood him, all restaurants were open to all employees, with possibly two or three exceptions.

One of the earlier Corporation restaurants was that operated by the Gary works of the American Sheet and Tin Plate Company. This restaurant was located in a separate brick building with concrete floor and steel peak roof; would serve 72 persons at one time; was well equipped; cost with equipment $7,300; and prior to the war served a dinner of soup, meat, two or three vegetables, bread and butter, and dessert for twenty-five cents. During the war the price of this dinner was advanced to thirty cents and has remained there. The restaurant also had *a la carte* service.

In its *Bulletin Number Seven* of 1918, the Bureau set forth " some fundamentals necessary for the successful operation of plant restaurants ". Briefly, these were: that the restaurant should be conveniently located, attractive in appearance, well lighted and perfectly clean; that service should be prompt, to secure which it recommended the cafeteria plan; that the food should be of the best quality, fresh, well cooked, served in an appetizing manner, of limited but sufficient variety; that the price of the food should be only its actual cost, but that this cost should be computed to include interest on the investment in the building, replacement of equipment, depreciation, and operating expenses; that payment for food should be by meal ticket or checks purchased in advance; and that the management should be responsible to the company in the same way as any other department of the plant. On January 1, 1924, the subsidiaries of the Corporation were operating 66 restaurants and lunch rooms. These were in addition to the boarding houses erected in some places by the Corporation.

A discussion of company housing concludes this section on community health work. To go back to the beginning of housing in the iron and steel industry would take us back at least to 1850 and possibly earlier. Individual companies, now parts of the Corporation, certainly did housing work as far back as the eighties. These earlier efforts have not been investigated in any detail but the evidence at hand shows fairly plainly that " shacking " or " shantying " would probably be a better term for them than housing.

The greatest development by the United States Steel Corporation has naturally been in the mining towns of its coal and iron subsidiaries and in such places as Gary, where the plant formed the nucleus for a town in what had formerly been more or less a desert. *Bulletin Number Seven* of the Bureau of Safety contains a number of pages devoted to the layout of some of the towns constructed wholly or largely as a Corporation venture, pictures of the houses, floor plans, etc., etc. Most of these data, while interesting and showing considerable appreciation of town-planning and good construction of individual houses, are unsatisfactory in some respects. For example, there are numerous references to the differences between the " better type " houses and the " low rental " houses provided for unskilled labor, but it has been impossible to secure directly from the office of the Corporation data on rents, leases, and other matters which explain exactly what these differences are. In one case, however, the Corporation has supplied figures of this sort to the Bureau of Labor Statistics which were not covered up in presentation. The objection to them is that they represent the best piece of work done in the housing program, and hence are not typical. Nevertheless, since they are detailed and fairly complete, they offer the most profitable basis for a discussion of the Corporation's work that is available, and will be summarized from the *Monthly Labor Review* for April, 1918. In that issue is a full description of the Corporation's town of Morgan Park, Minnesota. Though it was not intended to be a separate town, rather a suburb of Duluth, it has so far been maintained as a separate entity with no government and with only those functions of a government in operation which the Corporation has seen fit to establish.

The first work on the town site proper was begun in August, 1913. At that time Morgan Park was nothing more than fields and thickets, but by August, 1915, the first group of houses, a total of 349 dwellings, had been completed. After this first construction was carried through by the Minnesota Steel Company, a new subsidiary of the Corporation, the Morgan Park Company, was organized in the latter part of 1915 to take over the project. The effect of the development upon land values is shown by the facts that in 1906 before the steel plant was started the land now in the Park sold for $59.00 an acre, whereas in 1917 its selling value was about $1,975 an acre.

The better type of houses were built on the east side of the town on the shore of Spirit Lake; the row houses for the lower paid, unskilled labor on the west. Contrary to the provisions of the house-owning plan to be explained shortly, no land or house in Morgan Park has been sold to anyone. However, plans are now under consideration which would change this and permit the employees to own their homes here as they do in other Corporation towns. Because the title has been held by the Morgan Park Company, it has installed and operated an electric light plant, a system of daily collection of garbage and rubbish, street cleaning, snow removal, fuel distribution, policing, and a dual water system: one for drinking purposes from springs, and the other for sprinkling, sanitary fixtures, and fire purposes from the lake. All gas, water, and sewer mains are laid in alleys, and because of the severity of the climate, the latter two are put seven feet underground. All wiring, except the street-car trolley, is underground.

The so-called " low rental " or row houses for the lower-paid workmen are not continuous rows for an entire square but are separated into blocks containing four or more dwellings. The whole group of forty-two dwellings was constructed under a single contract in 1916 and 1917 at an average cost of $1,680 a dwelling, or $400 a room, not including bathrooms as separate rooms. Of the forty-two there are twenty-six with four rooms each, which may be grouped as follows: twelve heated by stoves renting for $10 a month; twelve heated by a furnace on the first floor renting for $11 a month; and two heated by a furnace in the basement renting for $12 a month. Of the fourteen dwellings having six rooms each, eight are heated by stoves, four by a furnace on the first floor, and two by a furnace in the basement. They rent for $15, $16.50, and $18.75, respectively. There is one double house with five rooms for each family, heated by a basement furnace, and renting for $13.75 a side.

The facts on the better class of houses are more detailed and hence are presented in tabular form on page 166.

In addition to these houses there are three boarding houses for single men and women, both skilled and unskilled, which are operated by the Morgan Park Company.

It will be noted that of the total of 437 houses, 395 are denominated as better class houses and only 42 as " low' rental " houses designed for unskilled labor. When the rents are examined, however, some of this difference seems to vanish, for of the so-called better houses a total of 140, or more than a third, rented for $15 a month; whereas eight

TABLE XIV

Cost and Rentals of better class of houses, Morgan Park.[1]

Type of house	No. of dwellings erected.	Cost per dwelling	Rooms per dwelling	Cost per Room	Rent per month
Houses constructed in 1914–1915:					
Single, detached	30	$3,353	5	$671	$20
	39	3,702	6	617	24
	10	5,592	8	699	32
Flat, detached	40	2,741	4	685	15
	70	2,850	5	570	20
Flat, double detached...	20	2,544	4	565	15
	20	2,544	5	565	20
Row, 4 dwellings to row.	60	2,144	4	536	15
6 dwellings to row ...	60	2,008	4	502	15
Total or Average....	349	$2,753	4.7	$588	$18
Houses constructed in 1916–17:					
Single, detached	7	5,750	5	1,150	28
	2	5,750	5	1,150	35
	4	6,450	6	1,075	35
	3	6,050	6	1,008	32
	4	6,050	6	1,108	35
	4	6,750	6	1,125	40
	4	7,750	7	1,107	40
	2	8,550	7	1,221	45
	7	8,390	8	1,049	50
	9	8,417	9	935	50
Total or Average...	46	$7,163	6.8	$1,049	$40
Grand Total.......	395				

of the low rental houses rented for $15, four for $16.50,
and two for $18.75. This means that fourteen of the low
rental houses, or exactly thirty-three and one-third per cent
of them, rented for as much as or more than the amounts

[1] *Monthly Labor Review*, April, 1918, p. 13.

received on thirty-five per cent of the better houses. These rents were of 1918. Most of them were raised in 1920.

Of the 3,000 individuals employed in Corporation plants in and around Duluth some thirty-five per cent are living in Corporation houses. This is well over the average for housing in the iron and steel industry in general, for the Bureau of Labor Statistics Bulletin No. 263 on *Housing by Employers in the United States* (p. 11) shows that of the 116,904 employees of the companies reporting in the northern district only 17.9 per cent were living in company houses. In the Birmingham district in Alabama of 3,180 employees, 29.2 per cent lived in company houses. The manager of the Bureau of Safety would make no estimate of the percentage of the Corporation's total employees who are housed in company houses, but from the facts that are available it is fairly easy to compute that it varies by districts in close conformity with the figures just cited for the industry in general.

Other towns that have been built by the Corporation or one of its subsidiaries are: Wilson Station, Pennsylvania; Westfield, Alabama; Chickasaw, Alabama; Lynch, Kentucky; South Donora, Pennsylvania; Gary, West Virginia; Gary, Indiana; McDonald, Ohio; Farrell, Pennsylvania. This list is by no means complete, particularly excluding housing projects carried on by some companies before they became subsidiaries of the Corporation. None of the towns is the equal of Morgan Park. It should be added that housing activities have not been confined to new communities though they have doubtless had their greatest development there; houses are being constructed or bought for employees in previously established towns.

Because of the refusal of the Corporation to supply any other figures on its houses and rentals it is impossible to reach any more satisfactory conclusions than the following:

First, the Corporation had constructed by January 1, 1924,

28,451 dwellings and boarding houses which were leased to its employees. These were principally in the mining towns and only about 10,000 of them were available for *bona fide* steel workers.

Second, the Corporation deserves considerable credit for keeping down rents and preventing speculation in the Morgan Park district of Duluth.

Third, Margaret Byington in her volume in the Pittsburgh Survey states that the houses " owned and rented by the Carnegie Land Company [a subsidiary of the Corporation] in Munhall are the best houses for the money in the town " in spite of the fact that they are " built in solid rows and wearisomely uniform ".[1]

Fourth, a comparison of the figures for Morgan Park with those for company housing in general as set forth in the government publication previously cited shows the following facts to be true. The construction, all-concrete, of the houses in Morgan Park is much better and more substantial than the great majority of company houses. (This construction is practically necessitated by the severe winters and is, of course, much better than that at most of the Corporation towns.) The rents in Morgan Park, figured on the basis of the monthly rental per house or per room, are much higher than for company houses on the whole. For example, Morgan Park has a little over 200 four-room houses. The lowest rent on these houses, and it applies to only 6 per cent of them, is $10 a month. Of the 17,643 four-room houses scheduled in the government investigation, 16,224, or 92 per cent of the total, rented for less than $10 a month. Again, the government figures show that only 3.5 per cent of the company houses in the scope of the survey rented for $18 or more a month. It happens that

[1] Byington, *op. cit.*, p. 48.

not a single house in Morgan Park rents for precisely $18, but almost exactly 50 per cent rent for more than $18. On the other hand, when rents are computed as a gross return on the amount invested, the Morgan Park Company receives 7.8 per cent on the 349 better class houses constructed in 1914 and 1915, 6.8 per cent on the 46 better class houses constructed in 1916 and 1917, and 8.9 per cent on the low rental houses, as compared with the 8.3 per cent secured by the sample of sixty companies doing housing on which the Bureau of Labor Statistics based its computations for company housing in general.[1]

More profitable comparisons than those made perhaps would be a comparison of Morgan Park with some other single community of similar construction, location, etc., and a comparison of the housing projects of the Corporation as a whole with the government report on all housing. The first has been impossible because of my failure to discover a community in which all conditions were sufficiently analagous to those in Morgan Park to validate conclusions; the second is not feasible because of the refusal of the Corporation to make public exhaustive figures on its rents, leases, and other details of the housing program.[2]

In addition to the housing projects in which dwellings are rented to the employees, the Corporation in the spring of 1920 put into effect a home-owning plan as a model for the subsidiaries. Prior to that time most of the companies were

[1] *Cf.* on this section the *Monthly Labor Review*, vol. 6, pp. 729-753 (April, 1918) with U. S. Bureau of Labor Statistics, Bul. No. 263, *Housing by Employers in the United States* (Washington, 1920), pp. 11, 14, 50, 133, 150, 186.

[2] The chief reason for this refusal was that it would enable the tenants to make comparisons without realizing the differences, such as the costs of building in different places at different times, and consequently, would involve the Corporation in countless explanations and discussions with its tenants that it did not desire to enter into.

operating similar plans but the Corporation was not satisfied with some of them and in particular desired to secure more uniformity. The details of the Corporation's plan as set forth by Mr. Close in an address to the American Iron and Steel Institute on May 28, 1920, are as follows:

A. Installment Payment Plan for an Existing Dwelling

This plan applied only to an existing dwelling owned by the Company, or bought by the Company from a private owner for an employee. The dwelling will be sold to employee under a contract providing for an initial payment of not less than ten per cent. of the purchase price; the balance of the purchase price to be paid in monthly installments extending over a period not exceeding ten to fifteen years, with interest on deferred payments at the rate of five (5%) per cent. per annum. The purchaser may anticipate payments at any time and is offered special inducements for early completion of contract. The title to the property remains in the Company until the completion on the contract. If, at any time, he desires to withdraw from the contract, he is permitted to do so and receive back all money he has paid on principal and interest thereon, plus five (5%) per cent. interest thereon less a rental which is based on 8% per annum of the purchase price for the period of possession.

B. Installment Payment Plan for Building a Dwelling

Under this plan the Company will build a dwelling for employee, title being taken in the name of the Company. The Company will furnish free plans and specifications and supervise the construction of the house. The dwelling will be sold to the employee under the same plan as outlined under "A," [except that the initial payment shall be not less than fifteen per cent of the purchase price.]

C. Mortgage Plan

This plan will best apply where purchaser is able to make a large initial payment and desires to have the title to the property in his own name. A loan not exceeding 75% of the cost of the property will be made to the employee, secured by a first mortgage bearing interest at 5% per annum. The loan may be repaid in installments. This plan may apply to sales of existing dwellings as well as to houses to be built.[1]

The final item in the housing program is the establishment of practical housekeeping centers. This work was begun a little over ten years ago and is concentrated largely in the southern subsidiaries. The Corporation states that their "purpose is to furnish an object lesson for the wives and daughters by illustrating what may be accomplished in the way of convenience, comfort and attractiveness within their means."[2] Some of the activities carried on at these centers are:

1. Classes for children in sewing, cooking and house-keeping.
2. Meetings for women with instructions in the care of infants, cooking, sewing, public health, and hygiene.
3. Clubs for small girls.
4. Clubs for boys, often a troop of Boy Scouts.
5. Clubs for women, social purposes.

The education and Americanization program of the Corporation naturally divides itself into two major parts: the night classes conducted for the employees in the plants, the Y. M. C. A., or in public schools, in which cases the Corporation bears all or most of the expense; and, second, the financial aid given to the public schools of certain communities.

Though the inauguration of the former plan is hard to date precisely, some work was done as early as 1906 in the American Bridge Company. The Corporation's claim that

[1] Close, *op. cit.*, p. 42.
[2] *Ibid.*, p. 24.

the classes are designed to meet the needs of any one in the plant who is anxious to learn a little more seems well founded, for everything from the alphabet to calculus and bridge engineering is taught. However, as might well be expected, the chief emphasis in the work has been laid upon English classes for foreigners and technical classes for those who wish such training. The work among the foreigners has consisted in teaching them to speak, read, and write the English language first and later to master a little simple arithmetic, American history, and civics. In the past few years there has been more and more emphasis on the last point. Since the Corporation wishes these men to become American citizens it has distributed pamphlets explaining the steps in taking out citizenship papers and has encouraged the men to take out their papers. The courses offered to those who are English-speaking include mechanical drawing, chemistry, steam, bridge, and electrical engineering, mathematics, physics, sheet-metal pattern drafting, plan reading, commercial geography, mining, government, business correspondence, salesmanship, etc., etc. In connection with these classes, several of the plants have developed fairly substantial libraries, largely technical in nature, from which the employees are allowed to draw books for home use. The assistant manager of the Bureau of Safety estimated that between ten and twenty per cent of the Corporation's employees were enrolled in these classes at any given time.[1]

----

[1] It would be most interesting to ascertain the percentage of the men needing this instruction in English who take it, and the percentage of those registering for it who complete their courses, but the former is obviously impossible and the Corporation as a whole has not compiled the latter. It is apparent, however, that a large majority of the foreigners needing the instruction most were, prior to August, 1923, working such long hours that they could not derive much benefit from the classes. Some indication of the situation is to be found in the statement . of A. H. Wyman of the Carnegie Steel Company to the National Asso-

The second development, Corporation participation in
common school education, has gone farthest perhaps in the
communities dependent upon the various plants of the Tennessee Coal, Iron, and Railroad Company in Alabama. For
some years this had been done in a somewhat desultory
fashion, but in 1913 an educational department was organized and the work carried on in a systematic manner. The
Company has aided in building schools in many cases and in
a few has constructed them entirely without county or state
aid. It makes a regular practice of supplementing salaries
in order to secure better teachers. In connection with its
public health work it has instituted regular medical inspection of the school children and the " tooth-brush drill " mentioned in another connection.

An entirely different phase of the welfare program, the
recreational facilities provided by the Corporation for its
employees, cannot be adequately treated here for the reason
that such treatment would entail a fairly lengthy paper in
itself. Some subsidiaries had made more progress than
others in providing recreational facilities at the time the
Corporation began to extend its supervision over the matter,
and even now some companies are well in the lead of others,
but undoubtedly there has been a tendency toward expansion and standardization in which the leaders have set the
mark. The Bureau's summary list of such installations
and facilities on January 1, 1924, shows among other
items 175 playgrounds, 125 athletic fields, 112 tennis courts,
19 swimming pools, and 21 band stands. That the children
of the neighborhood enjoy and utilize the playgrounds is

ciation of Corporation Schools in 1919 that of the thousands of workmen in South Chicago eligible for these classes only 341 registered,
and of these 169, or forty-seven per cent, failed to complete them because of reasons connected with hours. (Quoted in Interchurch, *Report
on the Steel Strike of 1919*, p. 82.)

established by the fact that the average daily attendance at all the playgrounds during the summer months has grown from 8,688 in 1913 to approximately 25,000 in 1924. Many of these playgrounds have been located in congested centers in Pittsburgh and other steel towns so that they may be looked upon in one sense as a part of the Corporation's accident prevention policy.

The athletic fields are to the older boys and men what the playgrounds are to the children. For both facilities the equipment varies greatly from place to place, but in several cases the athletic fields are equal, if not superior, to those of most of our smaller colleges or minor league baseball clubs.

In addition to the items listed, practically every plant now maintains an orchestra, band, glee club, or other musical organization. In most cases the company provided the majority of the instruments and continues to make regular contributions to aid in purchasing music and maintaining equipment. In some plants the bands give noon concerts twice or three times a week; at others the concerts are given in the evening.

A fairly recent development is the establishment of some forty clubs in the various subsidiaries. The usual practice has been for the company to build and equip the club-house, pay the taxes and insurance, and furnish heat, while the members pay all other expenses from the monthly dues ranging from twenty-five cents to one dollar. The most important features of these clubs are the dormitory facilities, reading rooms and libraries, gymnasiums, bowling alleys, basketball floors, swimming pools and baths, auditoriums and dance halls. Entertainments of various sorts ranging from educational lectures to purely social affairs are frequent throughout the year.[1]

[1] *Senate Hearings*, 1919, p. 263.

Savoring somewhat more of work than of recreation is the development of gardens under stimulus of company prizes, free seed, free plowing, or other inducements. This can be traced back certainly as far as 1904 when the United States Coal and Coke Company put some land under fence to be used for community gardens. This work has expanded steadily until now at most of the subsidiaries unoccupied land near the plant is plowed and fertilized at company expense and plots assigned to employees who wish to utilize them. In some subsidiaries the employees are encouraged to utilize whatever space their back lots afford, but in others, according to a former employee, this is so far from true that the company prohibits them from planting anything in any part of their yards and even from making a flower bed or a window box without securing special permission from the company. The bulletins of the Bureau of Safety contain no comprehensive or systematic data on the development of this work over a period of years and consequently the following facts are more suggestive than informing.

The 180 gardens at two of the mines of the United States Coal and Coke Company in 1914 produced vegetables worth $11,605. By 1918 there were 1,938 gardens aggregating 176 acres in the one town of Gary, West Virginia, with a product valued at something over $100,000. The H. C. Frick Coke Company reported 6,636 gardens cultivated by their employees in 1914 with an estimated value of produce of $142,536.20. The report for 1918 showed a value of $299,313.22 for this company. The Tennessee Coal, Iron and Railroad Company increased the number of its gardens from 771 in 1910 to 2,167 in 1914. The only totals available for the entire Corporation were for 1920, and from the nature of things could be little more than estimates. They showed that over 3,000 acres were under cultivation that summer and that the value of the produce was approximately a million dollars.

The development of these gardens caused the introduction by the Oliver Mining Company of Minnesota of an entirely new feature into its welfare program: the vegetable cellar. In the summer and fall of 1917 it constructed eight of these cellars and has operated them since that time with no charge to its employees. Though no artificial heat is used, a temperature above freezing is maintained so that vegetables may be kept through the winter and spring and into the early summer.

In addition to this very practical matter of vegetable gardens the Corporation has devoted some attention to the development and encouragement of flower gardens and lawns. Here, of course, the principal method of securing the desired results was the establishment of a series of cash prizes for the best-kept lawns. The success of such a project as this is largely a relative matter, but from the growth of the practice it is evident that the subsidiaries must consider it satisfactory.[1]

The origin of the Pension Fund in a gift from Mr. Carnegie and a later gift from the Corporation has been explained. The regulations governing the granting of pensions are set forth in detail in a pamphlet, *Pension Rules,* published by the Corporation. Briefly, they are as follows:

(a) Compulsory retirement for men at 70 years of age and for women at 60 after 25 years of service.

(b) Retirement at request of employee or his employing officer after age of 65 for men and 55 for women, after 25 years of service.

(c) Retirement by reason of permanent total incapacity after 15 years of service.

---

[1] U. S. Steel Corporation, Bureau of Safety, *Bulletin Number Five* (New York, 1914), pp. 58-70; *Bulletin Number Seven,* pp. 43-54; *Bulletin Number Eight,* p. 45.

(d) Pension basis: for each year of service, 1 per cent of average monthly earnings for the last 10 years of service. For example, a man who has worked 25 years, in the last 10 of which he averaged $60 a month, would receive 25% of 60, or $15 a month.

(e) Credit for service rendered to any of the plants of the subsidiary companies of the U. S. Steel Corporation or to the predecessors of such companies.

(f) Minimum pension $12.00 a month; maximum, $100.00 a month.

Other regulations of considerable significance include the following:

Employees who voluntarily quit the service will lose credit for all previous service. Employees who are discharged [does not include lay-off due to reduction of force] from the service will lose credit for all previous service, unless re-employed within six (6) months.

Pensions may be withheld or terminated in case of misconduct on the part of the beneficiaries, or for other cause sufficient in the judgment of the Board of Directors to warrant such action.

The Manager of the Fund shall decide all questions arising out of the administration of the fund and relating to employees, subject to a right of appeal to the Board of Directors. . . . The action of the Board of Directors or of any committee designated by the Board to hear such appeals shall be final and conclusive.[1]

On January 1, 1924, there were 4,054 pensioners.

The final item of the welfare program to be discussed is the one taken up first in the historical sketch of the development of the system. This change in the order of the presentation of the stock subscription plan has been made because,

---

[1] U. S. Steel Corporation, *Pension Rules* (New York, 1921) *passim*.

as pointed out before, it has always been more or less a thing apart from the rest of the program, and because there is a possibility that it should not be included under our definition of welfare work. Since, on the other hand, there is ground for the view that it is a part of the program and since the Corporation has listed the " cost of the employees' stock subscription plan " among its " expenditures for welfare " it is here included.

The stock subscription plan, or profit-sharing scheme as it is sometimes incorrectly termed, actually went into operation in the opening months of 1903 and has been continued to date. In spite of several changes made in the administrative details, the essential features of the plan have remained about as follows:

Each year the Corporation buys a number of its own shares and offers them to its employees at the purchase price. The kind of stock offered has varied a great deal during the twenty years, but it is accurate to say in general that during the first third of that period, with the exception of 1909, only preferred was sold, that during the second third both common and preferred were usually sold, and that of late years only common has been available. The number of shares which an individual may purchase varies with the amount of his annual salary, but a relatively greater proportion may be taken by the more poorly paid man in spite of the fact that absolutely his subscription is narrowly limited. Payments have to be made in monthly installments of not less than two dollars a share nor more than twenty-five per cent of the monthly earnings, such payments to be deducted from the subscriber's pay. Five per cent interest is charged for deferred payments. Prior to 1924, in addition to whatever dividends were declared, the subscriber to the stock received a premium, usually $5 but sometimes less, a share in January of each of the first five years that he retained the stock, remained in the employ of the Corporation, and showed " a proper interest in its welfare and progress ". Beginning with subscriptions made in 1924, however, the premium will be paid as follows: $3 the first year, $4 the second, $5 the third, $6 the fourth, and $7 the fifth. Those premiums which are forfeited for one reason or another are paid into a special fund that is credited with five per cent interest a year. " The Corporation will then by its own final determination award to each subscriber whom it shall find deserving thereof as many parts of such accumulated fund as he shall be entitled to on the basis of the number of shares then held by him under this plan." [1] After this if the subscriber continues to hold his stock he receives only the regular dividends.

That this plan is financially advantageous to the employees is apparent at a glance, but just how advantageous it is becomes much more clear when its returns are set down in dollars and in percentages. The first extra dividend was declared in January, 1908. By that time of the 26,399 employees who had subscribed in 1903 for 47,551 shares only 5,409 holding 12,339 shares remained. The extra dividend amounted to $65.04 a share. In 1909 it was $19.10 and in 1910, $16.80. During these five-year periods the subscribers had received regular dividends of $7.00 a share and the premium of $5.00 for retaining the share. These two items made a return of $60.00 a share for the period. Adding the extra dividends for the five-year periods ending with 1907, 1908, and 1909 to this gives a return on each share bought in 1903 of $125.04, on each share bought in

---

[1] This phraseology has recurred in the annual circular letter to employees and has been often quoted. At the time Mr. Fitch was preparing his volume in the Pittsburgh Survey the Corporation provided him with a copy of several of these circular letters which are reproduced in *The Steel Workers* and from which this quotation is made. (p. 316).

1904 of $79.10, and on each share bought in 1905 of $76.10. These shares were bought at $82.50, $55.00, and $87.50, respectively. Consequently, the net return in five years on the 1903 investment was 142.9 per cent; on the 1904, 143.8 per cent; on the 1905, 86.97 per cent. The average yearly return was 28.6 per cent, 28.7 per cent, and 17.4 per cent. In some years the return has not been so great but U. S. Steel bought on this plan is still a very good investment. The table on page 181 indicates the extent to which advantage has been taken of the offer by the indicated groups of employees.

Part of the changes between 1916 and 1921 are explained on the basis of the increases in wages, but, nevertheless, it is apparent that the highly skilled and supervisory elements are those most benefited. Moreover it is a self-evident proposition that it is more profitable to the employee to hold his stock for only five years and then to sell it and buy other stock on which he can draw the annual premiums and participate in the quinquennial division of forfeited premiums. These facts raise the question as to whether this is really a stock-owning plan or simply a method of holding employees, and particularly those skilled and trained employees who would be difficult to replace, to the Corporation. The attempt to answer this and similar questions it seems best to defer to the concluding chapter.

A complete record of the Corporation's expenditures for Welfare is not available but on pages 182-183 will be found a statement which covers the period from January 1, 1912, to January 1, 1924. As will be seen the Corporation uses the term welfare in this statement in a narrower sense than has been employed here. An examination of the quarterly " welfare record " sent in by each subsidiary to the Bureau of Safety shows that expenditures for the following items are charged to the welfare account: churches, schools, li-

TABLE XV

NUMBER OF EMPLOYEES SUBSCRIBING AND NUMBER OF SHARES TAKEN BY
WAGE GROUPS. U S. STEEL STOCK SUBSCRIPTION PLAN,
1903-1922 [1]

Year	Number of Employees Subscribing whose Annual Wage was			Number of Shares taken by Employees whose Annual Wage was		
	Less than $800	Between $800 and $2,500	Above $2,500	Less than $800	Between $800 and $2,500	Above $2,500
1903....	11,373	13,845	1,181	12,844	28,203	6,504
1904....	4,126	5,094	692	8,701	15,709	7,234
1905....	3,531	4,297	666	4,512	9,921	3,747
1906....	5,070	6,277	845	5,610	13,641	4,750
1907....	5,276	7,915	972	6,058	16,051	5,041
1908....	9,094	14,277	1,156	9,369	17,356	3,677
1909....	6,948	11,134	1,034	7,836	18,526	6,971
1910....	5,858	10,426	1,097	5,858	14,281	4,540
1911....	9,196	15,835	1,274	10,787	29,575	8,034
1912....	14,999	20,076	1,503	16,839	35,426	8,876
1913....	12,322	21,687	1,678	13,706	37,019	9,276
1914....	14,901	29,090	1,937	18,007	59,217	12,809
1915*...	......	.....	....	......	.....	......
1916....	7,015	16,011	1,605	8,648	31,528	9,362
1917....	3,127	32,654	2,545	3,127	51,618	11,774
1918....	1,774	35,635	4,581	2,085	70,022	21,378
1919†...	1,404	45,232	13,156	2,042	98,945	54,111
1920†...	553	42,851	19,867	562	88,159	72,466
1921†...	563	49,938	25,663	732	124,689	116,364
1922†...	1,010	26,154	6,711	1,287	58,683	33,315

* No offer made this year.

† Subject to revision within the five-year subscription term.

braries, clubs, restaurants and lunch rooms, rest and waiting rooms, playgrounds, swimming pools, athletic fields,
tennis courts, band stands, visiting nurses, practical house-
keeping centers, gardens, and pensions. From time to time
suspicions have arisen that other items were being charged

[1] These figures were supplied directly from the office of the Corporation. The 1923 data were withheld, however, for the reason explained in
the preface.

TABLE XVI

W<small>ELFARE</small> E<small>XPENDITURES</small>

	1912	1913	1914	1915	1916	1917
Welfare................	$1,068,253	$1,600,242	$535,056	$476,384	$752,114	$1,652,956
Sanitation.............	*	*	615,966	953,056	1,402,798	2,406,951
Accident prevention	595,649	660,593	565,334	608,644	848,079	998,806
Accident relief..........	2,203,099	2,564,839	1,861,476	1,694,465	2,292,956	2,769,451
Stock subscription	893,662	999,499	1,261,688	1,140,421	1,158,369	1,175,094
Pensions in excess of income from permanent fund	132,479	159,306	216,954	335,970	361,988	339,093
Creation of permanent pension fund	500,000	500,000	500,000	500,000	500,000	500,000
Total	$5,393,142	$6,484,479	$5,556,474	$5,708,940	$7,316,304	$9,842,351
Total pension payments.	$358,780	$422,815	$511,967	$659,389	$711,130	$712,506
Additional benefit payments and administration cost	56,175	43,222	35,621	32,874	32,032	30,762

to this account on which there was room for considerable difference of opinion as to whether or not they were really " welfare " expenditures.   During the Congressional investigation in 1911, Chairman Stanley of the House Committee asked G. W. Perkins of the Corporation the following question: " You have a ' welfare ' fund.   I will ask you if you have not contributed regularly about $3,000 out of that welfare fund to the Protective Tariff League and your books show it to be a fact? " [1]   The minutes of the executive committee of the Corporation showed that such a contribution was made but not to what account it was charged. Mr. Perkins facetiously remarked that another contribution of $3,000 made on January 17, 1911, to aid in financing a second edition of George P. Curtiss' *Protection and Pros-*

[1] *Stanley Hearings,* 1911, vol. ii, p. 1431.

U. S. Steel Corporation, 1912-1923 [1]

1918	1919	1920	1921	1922	1923	Total
$3,142,899	$2,523,523	$3,263,684	$3,106,059	$1,843,760	$2,418,014	$22,382,945
3,145,174	3,208,717	4,227,263	3,615,150	2,252,975	3,019,363	24,847,414
1,110,064	1,143,534	1,420,456	1,061,685	1,175,171	1,763,381	11,951,432
2,919,226	3,855,121	4,937,158	3,973,718	3,786,385	4,357,282	37,215,177
1,298,091	1,538,300	2,061,151	2,211,575	2,365,137	2,413,096	18,516,083
136,644	142,254	203,459	374,691	694,942	875,080	3,972,860
5,000,000	......	......	......	......	......	8,000,000
$16,752,098	$12,411,449	$16,113,171	$14,342,878	$12,118,370	$14,846,216	$126,885,911
$709,059	$733,707	$779,766	$947,879	$1,267,661	$1,447,112	$9,261,771
31,424	31,867	36,020	34,820	35,668	36,376	436,861

perity " should have been charged to Welfare Work. We do a great deal of that." [2] It is fairly evident that some of the committee members did not take the matter so lightly. The changes in the table over the period of ten years show that the Corporation has made some concessions to critics of its accounting. The center of attack has apparently been the inclusion of administrative expenses under " welfare expenditures," " expenditures for improving the conditions of employees," or similar captions. At any rate there have been two revisions of figures, one to eliminate the administrative costs of the pension system, another for the same purpose in the item of relief. The result is that over $6,000,000 that would have been included by the 1910

[1] In 1912 and 1913 " sanitation " was included in " welfare."
[2] *Stanley Hearings*, 1911, vol. ii, p. 1431.

methods of computation are left out under those of 1922. Even at that the Corporation has spent $127,000,000 in its welfare work since 1911 and a good many millions before that date.

These, then, are the facts of the Corporation's welfare program: so many millions of dollars spent, so many lives saved through the safety campaign, so many men trained in various ways, so many installations of one sort or another. But the facts themselves are not sufficient. Why does the Corporation spend these millions? How does this program affect the daily lives of the Corporation's employees? In short, what does it mean? To these questions and to others raised by the facts previously presented the next chapter attempts to make answer.

CHAPTER VII

Summary and Conclusions

In attempting to formulate conclusions on the labor policy of the United States Steel Corporation the writer pretends to positive certainty on only one point, viz., that whatever is said will be severely criticized. The American Federation of Labor convention of 1909 denounced the Corporation as the " greatest enemy " of organized labor; the Corporation officials pride themselves on treating their employees as well or better than labor was ever treated in any line of industry " at any period in the history of the world in any country; " Mr. Fitch states that certain aspects of the Corporation's policy led to such " repression " of its men as to cause him to " doubt whether you could find a more suspicious body of men than the employees of the United States Steel Corporation;" the Interchurch Commission was most emphatic in its condemnation of the excessive hours demanded, the inadequate wages paid, and the " no-conference " attitude of the Corporation; and A. Cotter's opinion is sufficiently explicit in the title of his book, *U. S. Steel: A Corporation with a Soul.* To these expressions might be added countless others on both sides of the controversy, but they are sufficient to make the point. Despite the possible presumptuousness of adding other comment on a topic so fully covered, I summarize my conclusions on the character of the labor policy of the United States Steel Corporation in two words: paternalistic and autocratic—paternalistic primarily in its welfare program, and autocratic in its method of fixing wages and hours and in handling grievances.

The discussion of the Corporation's welfare work in the preceding two chapters is sufficiently detailed to make it clear that the term paternalistic is not used with any invidious connotations. When an industrial corporation takes care of its injured employees free of charge in its hospitals, maintains a corps of visiting nurses, provides playgrounds, tennis courts, swimming pools and athletic fields, subsidizes schools, and institutes a " tooth-brush drill " for the children of its employees, it is difficult to deny that such a corporation is acting *in loco parentis*. But if this is all that need be said concerning the welfare work, why is it so often contemptuously referred to by critics both within and without the organization as a " toilets policy " or " hell-fare work " ?

The chief reason seems to be that these critics do not believe that the program really is one of " welfare; " on the contrary, they have convinced themselves that every item in the program is either a part of the Corporation's system of maintaining a nonunion organization, or a commercial proposition from which dividends are to be reaped as from any other investment. The second of these motives is, of course, not denied *in toto*, nor is there any reason for denying it; but Corporation officials object to the emphasis laid upon this interpretation of the program. Although they are far from pretending that their motives are altogether altrusitic, they feel entitled to some credit which many critics seem unwilling to give.

The notion that welfare is only a part of the anti-union campaign is, perforce, denied, since the Corporation maintains that it " does not combat unions as such." The evidence that to my mind disproves this contention has been stated. The question remains as to whether any part of the welfare program is or can be used to combat unions. To the possibility of such use there is only one answer: without doubt any part of the plan or all of it can be used in checking unions, if only by removing sources of dissatisfaction, such as unsanitary conditions in a plant, and by creating a sentiment among the men that " the company is a good outfit to work for, after all." And to such use no exception could be taken, of course, if the labor policy of the Corporation at other points met the legitimate expectations of the employees. But this, as has been shown at length, it fails to do. It is a legitimate claim of workmen to bargain collectively concerning wages, hours, and conditions of work. This claim the Corporation refuses. Moreover, since housing programs furnish ideal weapons for crushing organization campaigns, in localities where a considerable portion of the Corporation's employees live in company houses those employees can not be as independent as if they were living in their own homes. Even more obviously available for fighting unions and for limiting independence and initiative is the stock subscription plan. As previously explained the buyer gains most, not by retaining his shares permanently, but by holding them no more than the five years during which he receives extra dividends and accumulates an interest in the fund created by the failure of some subscribers to qualify for the extra dividends. In order to qualify the subscriber must have been " continuously in the employ " of the Corporation or one of its subsidiaries in the year preceding the payment of the extra dividend and must have " shown a proper interest in its welfare and progress," or, as otherwise stated in the 1909 circular, must exhibit " a letter from a proper official showing that he has worked to promote the best interests of the company." It is difficult for anyone who has studied the history of the Corporation to believe that such a letter would be given to a man who was in any way " contaminated " with unionism. It is even more difficult for anyone to study this particular scheme without realizing that it is something more than a pure stock-owning proposition.

Permanent retention of the stock is not encouraged; on the contrary there is a high premium on a policy of rapid turn-over of the shares. But this rapid turn-over of shares is not calculated to result in a similarly rapid turn-over of men; on the contrary again it is admirably calculated to hold men in the employ of the Corporation and to make them less willing to take any action the Corporation officials are likely to construe as not conducive to the " welfare and progress " of the Corporation.

The pension system, likewise, obviously exercises a restraining influence upon the workmen's initiative and independence. It will be recalled that in addition to other limitations the administrators of the system reserved the power to withhold or terminate pensions in case of " misconduct " or any other cause deemed sufficient. Since men were regularly discharged for joining a union, prospective pensioners would be most likely to hesitate a long time before prejudicing their chances for a pension by taking any action that might be disapproved by the officials. Further rewards the " loyal " employee finds in other features of the welfare program, features that may be accurately described as paternalistic.

The second characterization applied to the Corporation's labor policy is that it is autocratic, chiefly in the determination of wages and hours and in the disposition of grievances of all sorts. Is this characterization accurate? In answering the question the reader must review the evidence presented.

The sections dealing with hours of labor were little more than a history of the seven-day week and the twelve-hour day. The Corporation having kept no adequate record of either, it was necessary to secure most of the data from the reports of sundry investigations. It will be recalled that the Corporation has " eliminated " the seven-day week on at

least three occasions, but that as recently as the spring of
1924 this schedule still prevailed in certain departments of
the Edgar Thomson works at Braddock. The orders of
1907 were " forgotten " in the boom of 1909; those of 1910
in the period of the war. Following the publication of Mr.
Fitch's " Old Age at Forty " a committee of stockholders
of the Corporation, appointed at the suggestion of Mr.
Charles M. Cabot, reported against the continuance of the
twelve-hour day, but nothing was done in the mills. From
time to time other investigators, both public and private,
pointed out the desirability of abolishing the long day.
Whatever else may or may not be true concerning the causes
of the strike of 1919, it cannot be denied that long hours
were a significant factor in forcing the issue. Through the
agency of the late President Harding a committee of the
American Iron and Steel Institute was appointed to consider
the possibility of abolishing the twelve-hour day. Its report was an indefinite postponement. Disapproval of the
decision was expressed by individuals in every walk of life
and by publications of every shade of opinion. Within
three months of indefinitely postponing the reform the Corporation had inaugurated it.

These are but the outstanding facts and a rereading of the
details previously presented will only strengthen the impression they convey. The Corporation has always subordinated
its interest in reforming hours to its interest in output and
profits. The reforms were not effected as the result of a
careful and scientific investigation by the Corporation. They
were not the result of an amicable agreement between employers and workmen. In every case they were forced by
the activities of " outsiders ", a business depression, or out-
raged public opinion.

The record on wages supports the same conclusion: the
labor policy of United States Steel is the policy of an

autocrat.   In England and in many industries in America wages are agreed upon by employers and employees, and in the former country in a large number of trades a legislative minimum is set below which wages can not be driven.   Until the close of the last century such legislation was probably unnecessary in this country because of the accessibility of free or very cheap land, but that situation has not obtained during the history of the United States Steel Corporation. In common with other employers it has taken advantage of the situation to pay to its common labor group wages that make such labor a single man's job.   Because of bad business conditions in 1903 the Corporation announced a wage cut, effective January 1, 1904, that further widened the gap between living costs and common labor's earnings, a gap not closed until the effect of war-time increases was felt in 1919.[1] Another bad year in 1921 brought a series of drastic cuts that tumbled the common labor rate from a high of forty-six cents with time and a half for time over eight hours in May to a low of thirty cents with no overtime in September. But the chief point here is, of course, not the adequacy of the wage but the manner in which it is determined.   That has always been by fiat of the executives, subject only to the exigencies of business.

But more illuminating than any other illustration of the Corporation's methods is that furnished by Judge Gary himself to the Senate Committee in 1919.

. . . Now then, sometimes there have been complaints made. For instance, to mention a somewhat trivial circumstance, some three or four years ago—not to be exactly specific as to date— one of our presidents telephoned to the president of our Corporation, who is in general charge of operations, that a certain number of men—it may have been a thousand or it may have

---

[1] *Cf.,* the table on p. 85.

been two thousand men—in a certain mill had all gone out, and his report was that there was no reason for their going out—

Senator Sterling. When you speak of "one of our presidents," you mean the president of a subsidiary company?

Mr. Gary. Yes; the president of a subsidiary company. And he said, "It is very easy for me to fill this mill, and I will proceed to do it." The president of the corporation came to me immediately and reported this. I said, "Tell him to wait and to come to New York." He came the next morning and he made substantially that same statement to me. I said, "Have you taken pains to find out; has anybody spoken to you?" "No," he said, "I have not received any complaint whatever." I said, "Are you sure no complaint has been made to anyone?" He said, "I will find out." I said, "You had better do so before you decide what you are going to do or what you propose to do." He went back; got hold of the foreman. A committee of men had come to the foreman and said that they thought three things, if I remember, were wrong —not very important, but they claimed they were wrong. And the president came back the second time and reported that; and I said, "Well, now, if they state the facts there, isn't the company wrong?" "Well," he said, "I don't consider it very important." I said, "That is not the question. Are you wrong in any respect? It seems to me you are wrong with respect to two of those things, and the other, not. Now, you go right back to your factory and just put up a sign that, with reference to those two particular things, the practice will be changed." [1]

Nothing could make clearer the lack of cooperation between bosses and men. The foreman had failed to pass on the complaint to his superior; the men had apparently failed to make a contact with anyone who would bring the matter to the attention of the president of the subsidiary; the president was willing to fill the places of these one or two thou-

[1] *Senate Hearings,* 1919, pp. 161-162.

sand men without making any investigation. Worst of all
was the solution: " just put up a sign! " In industries in
which the principle of collective bargaining is recognized
complaints are not handled in this summary fashion. Why
does not collective bargaining obtain in the plants of the
United States Steel Corporation? [1]

The obvious answer that the executives of the Corporation
do not believe in collective bargaining is true, but it is not
particularly illuminating, for it only raises another question:
why this unbelief? Part of the difficulty lies in the facts
summarized in the chapter on the attitude of the Corporation toward labor organizations. In the heyday of its power
the Amalgamated Association of Iron, Steel and Tin Workers was arrogant, short-sighted, and offensive. As pointed
out, the situation had become intolerable. The strength of
the union had to be mitigated to some extent. If the action
taken had been actually " mitigation " much subsequent un-
pleasantness might have been avoided, but the history of
the struggle was not such as to give much hope of modera-
tion on either side. The Homestead tragedy of 1892 was
only the most spectacular of the series of more or less disgraceful episodes that have characterized the feud. Each
side cited Homestead as a horrible example of the criminal
lengths to which the other was willing to go. With such a
background in the history of the most important constituents

---

[1] Corporation officials insist, of course, that complaints can be brought
to the proper authority by any one at any time. " Any employe or any
self-appointed group of employes from any department throughout our
large and diversified works and activities is at liberty at all times to
present to the respective foremen, and, if desired, to the higher appointees
or the officials all questions involving the interests and welfare of both
employe and employer for discussion and disposition. In this way fair
and satisfactory adjustments are made." (Pamphlet report of Judge
Gary's " Remarks " to the stockholders, April 19, 1920, p. 11). As a
matter of fact the incident related by Judge Gary to the Senate and
quoted in the text was intended to show how well this arrangement
functioned. To my mind it demonstrates the reverse.

of the new combination it was inevitable that the members
of the executive committee should unanimously express
themselves as " unalterably opposed to any extension of
union labor," and that they should in the first year of the
Corporation's history enter upon an anti-union campaign
that rapidly wiped out the organizations. That these men
honestly believed they were acting in the best interests of
their stockholders, their workmen, and economic society
there seems little reason to doubt. To repeat Mr. Gary's
statement to the stockholders at the meeting of May 18,
1921 :

Personally, I believe they [labor unions] may have been
justified in the long past, for I think the workmen were not
always treated justly; that because of their lack of experience
or otherwise they were unable to protect themselves; and
therefore needed the assistance of outsiders in order to secure
their rights.

But whatever may have been the conditions of employment
in the long past, and whatever may have been the results of
unionism, concerning which there is at least much uncertainty,
there is at present, in the opinion of the large majority of both
employers and employes, no necessity for labor unions; and
that no benefit or advantage through them will accrue to anyone except the union labor leaders.

Equally illuminating is the following extract from the
Senate Hearings in 1919 :

Senator Walsh. Now, I suppose you will agree that there
has been no force in America that has done more to shorten
the hours of labor—
Mr. Gary. To do what?
Senator Walsh. To increase wages, to better living conditions of the workmen, than organizations of labor.
Mr. Gary. I deny it positively, emphatically. I want to say
that the United States Steel Corporation has been in the van
all the time—

Senator Walsh. But I am speaking very generally and not about your organization. Has it not been because of the pressure upon legislators of organized labor bodies that has brought about the child labor laws, that has brought about the cutting down of the hours of labor for women and children, that has brought about the eight-hour working day, that has brought about the increase of wages, that has brought about better sanitary conditions and better home living conditions? Is not that the great factor that has been brought to bear upon the public that has influenced public opinion and also influenced public legislation? Has not that been the labor organizations?

Mr. Gary. I want to tell you, on the contrary, Senator, that where the labor unions have advocated these things you speak of they have followed the established practice of the United States Steel Corporation, as a rule.[1]

How many students of the labor movement and of the labor policies of the Corporation will agree with these statements by Judge Gary? In the business field he recognizes the need of combination. The Corporation itself is a gigantic example of the power that combination carries with it. Is not the refusal of such a combination to treat with its employees collectively through representatives of their own choosing clearly out of harmony with the spirit of the age? The reader's answer to this question in the light of the evidence presented must determine whether he approves the labor policies of the Corporation or believes that they should be modified in the direction made familiar in this country by the methods employed in the building industry and the printing industry where the employee's right to a voice in determining the conditions under which he works has long been recognized.

[1] P. 178.

BIBLIOGRAPHY

GENERAL

Albrecht, A. E., *International Seamen's Union of America*, Washington, 1923.

Bridge, J. H., *The Inside History of the Carnegie Steel Company*, New York, 1903.

Bureau of Applied Economics, *Standards of Living*, Bul. 7, Washington, 1920.

Byington, M. F., *Homestead: the Households of a Mill Town*, New York, 1910.

Chapin, R. C., *Standard of Living Among Workingmen's Families in New York City*, New York, 1909.

Close, C. L., *Welfare Work in the Steel Industry*, an address at the annual meeting of the American Iron and Steel Institute, New York, 1920.,

Cotter, A., *U. S. Steel: A Corporation with a Soul*, New York, 1921.

Eastman, Crystal, *Work-Accidents and the Law*, New York, 1910.

Federal Council of the Churches of Christ in America, *The Twelve Hour Day in the Steel Industry*, Bul. 3, New York, 1923.

Fitch, John A., *The Steel Workers*, New York, 1911.

Foster, Wm. Z., *The Grerat Steel Strike and its Lessons*, New York, 1920.

Gary, Elbert H., Addresses to Stockholders, to the Iron and Steel Institute, etc. (pamphlets).

Hearings before the Committee on Investigation of the United States Steel Corporation, 8 vols., Washington, 1911.

Hoagland, H. E., *Wage Bargaining on the Vessels of the Great Lakes*, Urbana, Ill., 1917.

Investigation of Strike in the Steel Industries, Hearings before the Committee on Education and Labor, 2 vols., Washington, 1919.

King, W. I., *Wealth and Income of the People of the United States*, New York, 1915.

More, Louise B., *Wage-Earners' Budgets*, New York, 1907.

Ogburn, W. F., " The Standard-of-living Factor in Wages ", *Papers and Proceedings of the Thirty-fifth Annual Meeting of the American Economic Association*, March, 1923.

Robinson, J. S., *Amalgamated Association of Iron, Steel and Tin Workers*, Baltimore, 1917.

Testimony before the Congressional Investigating Committee, Misc. Doc. No. 335, 52nd Cong., 1st Session.

U. S. Bureau of Labor Statistics:

Bul. 234, *The Safety Movement in the Iron and Steel Industry, 1907 to 1917*, Washington, 1918.

Bul. 250, *Welfare Work for Employees in Industrial Establishments in the United States*, Washington, 1919.

Bul. 263, *Housing by Employers in the United States*, Washington, 1920.

Bul. 272, *Workmen's Compensation Legislation in the United States and Canada, 1919*, Washington, 1921.

Bul. 298, *Causes and Prevention of Accidents in the Iron and Steel Industry, 1910-1919*, Washington, 1922.

Bul. 305, *Wages and Hours of Labor in the Iron and Steel Industry: 1907-1920*, Washington, 1922.

U. S. Bureau of the Census:

Census of Manufactures, Part I, 1905.

Abstract of Statistics of Manufacturing, 1909, 1914, 1919.

U. S. Steel Corporation, Bureau of Safety, Sanitation and Welfare:

Bulletins covering entire field, 1910 to 1924.

Pamphlets on some phase of the work such as pension rules, sanitary installation specifications, etc., etc.

Walker, C. R., *Steel, The Diary of a Furnace Worker*, Boston, 1922.

Williams, Whiting, *What's on the Worker's Mind*, New York, 1920.

REPORTS

Commission of Inquiry of the Interchurch World Movement:

Report on the Steel Strike of 1919, New York, 1920.

Public Opinion and the Steel Strike, New York, 1921.

Commissioner of Corporations, *Report of the Commissioner of Corporations on the Steel Industry*, Washington, 1911.

Commissioner of Labor, *Eighteenth Annual Report, Cost of Living and Retail Prices of Food*, Washington, 1903.

Commissioner of Labor, *Report on Conditions of Employment in the Iron and Steel Industry in the United States*, 4 vols., Washington, 1913.

Drury, H. B., " The Technique of Changing from the Two-Shift to the Three-Shift System in the Steel Industry," (Proof-sheets of May, 1922) Report to the Cabot Fund.

Federated American Engineering Societies, *The Twelve-Hour Shift in Industry*, Report of the Committee on Work-Periods in Continuous Industry, New York, 1923.

Final Report of Commission on Industrial Relations, Washington, 1915.

_owe, W. E., and Dohr, J. L., *Report on Analysis of Earnings and Disposition thereof of United States Steel Corporation* to the Director General of Railroads (mimeographed pamphlet).

Report of the Immigration Commission, *Immigrants in Industries*, part ii: *Iron and Steel Manufacturing*, Washington, 1911.

U. S. Steel Corporation, *Annual Reports*, 1902-1923, New York.

PERIODICALS

American Economic Review:
    Rubinow, I. M., "The Recent Trend of Real Wages," Dec. 1914.
    Douglas, P. H., and Lamberson, F., "The Movement of Real Wages," September, 1921.
    Stecker, M. L., "Family Budgets and Wages," September, 1921.

Bulletin of the Taylor Society, Drury, H. B., "The Three-Shift System in the Steel Industry," February, 1921.

Charities and the Commons, Commons, John R., "Wage Earners of Pittsburgh," March 6, 1909.

Iron Age, September 20, 1923; September 27, 1923; January 3, 1924.

Monthly Labor Review, April, 1918; October, 1919; February, 1924.

New York Times.

Political Science Quarterly, Moore, Henry L., "Employment and Wages," March, 1907.

Survey, November 8, 1919; March 5, 1921.

INDEX

Accidents, 148-150
Accident prevention, 143-152, 182
Accident relief, 151-155, 182
Amalgamated Association of Iron, Steel and Tin Workers, 24, 95, 96, 100, 101, 107, 115, 118, 192
American Federation of Labor: attempt to organize steel workers in 1919, 105-110
Americanization, 171

Blacklist, 125-127
Bonuses, 87
Budgets: comparison of with earnings of Corporation employees, 71-86

Cabot, Charles M.: efforts to reduce hours in Corporation plants, 26, 28
Cabot Fund, 34, 41, 42
Civil liberties: alleged abrogation of, 132-137
Close, C. L., 7; manager of Welfare Bureau, 142; comments on this study, 8; on carelessness of workmen, 143; on the housing program, 170; on the 7-day week, 35
Closing mills after signing scale for them, 100, 112
Collective bargaining, 192
Committee for Organizing Iron and Steel Workers, 105, 109, 134; on number of strikers in 1919, 110
Convict labor: use of to combat unions, 111-114
Cost of living, 65, 67, 85; see Budgets

Discharge for union activities, 120-125
Drury, Horace B., 41, 42, 53

Education: as part of welfare program, 171-173
199]

Eight-hour day, 24; adoption of in continuous processes in 1923, 49; experience of Colorado Fuel and Iron Company, 47; results of change to, 50

Federal Council of Churches: research bulletin on the 12-hour shift in industry, 48; statement on report of the committee of the Iron and Steel Institute on abolition of the 12-hour day, 45
Fitch, John A., 52, 89, 94, 185; investigation for Cabot Fund of hours in steel industry in 1920, 34, 39; on blacklisting, 125; on discharge for union activities, 122, 125; on spy system in Corporation plants, 115; on stock subscription plan, 179
Fitzpatrick, John, 107, 109, 133
Foreigners: alleged use of to combat unions, 127-130; proportion of in steel industry, 127
Foster, William Z., 103, 109; on the basic 8-hour day, 106; on causes of failure of 1919 strike, 110; on murder of Mrs. Snellings, 133; resolution favoring organization of steel workers, 105; secretary-treasurer of 1919 strike committee, 105

Gary, Elbert H.: on causes of 1919 strike, 103; on discharge for union activities, 120; on employment of foreigners, 130; on federal licensing of corporations, 54; on hours of labor, 26, 35, 37, 38, 39, 43, 49, 54; on methods of handling grievances, 190-192; on the murder of Mrs. Snellings, 134; on treatment of labor, 117; on unions, 93, 193; on wages, 86, 87; refusal to confer with strike leaders in 1919, 108

199